Cities
Transf

MORRIS JUPPENLATZ

in ormation

The Urban Squatter Problem
of the Developing World

UNIVERSITY OF QUEENSLAND
PRESS

Distributed in the United States by
CRANE, RUSSAK & COMPANY, INC.
347 Madison Avenue
New York, New York 10017

National Library of Australia Registry Number AUS 68-1229

SBN 7022 0571 0

Set in Baskerville 11/12 and printed on 100 gsm glazed Woodfree.
Printed and bound by Dai Nippon Printing Co. (International)
Ltd., Hong Kong

Designed by Cyrelle

Distributed by International Scholarly Book Services, Inc. Great
Britain – Europe – North America

"This natural inequality of the two powers of population, and of production in the earth, and that great law of our nature which must constantly keep their effects equal . . . No fancied equality, no agrarian regulations in their utmost extent, could remove the pressure of it even for a single century. And it appears, therefore, to be decisive against the possible existence of a society, all the members of which, should live in ease, happiness, and comparative leisure; and feel no anxiety about providing the means of subsistence for themselves and families."

Thomas Malthus, 1798
An Essay on the Principle of Population

Acknowledgments

To the United Nations Organization, the many studies, reports, and publications of which form the basic reference material for this book, the author makes a special acknowledgment.

For the facilities and details which made possible the writing of the section on New Delhi, the author is indebted to Mr. C.P. Patel, Director of the National Building Organization, New Delhi, to Mr. Ved Prakash, Associate Planning Commissioner, Delhi Development Authority, and to Mr. V.V. Bodas, Chief Architect-Planner, Municipal Corporation of Delhi, who conducted the author on a visual inspection of the *bustees* of Delhi.

The author also acknowledges his indebtedness to Mr. Donald Hanson, Inter-regional Adviser on Housing, United Nations Secretariat, for providing the published reports on the housing proposals of Turkey; to Mr. J. Frazer, Commissioner, Hong Kong Housing Authority, and to Mr. J.R. Firth, Chief Architect to the Authority, who in 1962 provided all the facilities for inspecting the squatter colonies and redevelopment projects and made available much of the detail which forms the basis of the section on Hong Kong; to Attorney J.S. de Vera, Assistant General Manager of the People's Homesite and Housing Corporation, and Mr. Felix Abesamis, Head of the Housing Research Team and subsequently Director of the Central Institute for the Training and Relocation of Urban

Squatters (CITRUS), for facilitating the writing of the section on the Philippines; to Father Alban Kelly, Carmelite Fathers, to Mother Superior Flavie, Sisters of Immaculate Conception, to Mr. Oscar Arellano, Executive Director, Operation Brotherhood International, and to Col. Jose Illustre and Mr. V. Palugod, both Field Co-ordinators of Sapang Palay Squatter Resettlement Project, from whom the author drew much inspiration for the section dealing with the squatter problem in the Philippines and the Sapang Palay squatter relocation project; to Dr. Otto Koenigsberger, Head of the Department of Tropical Studies, Architectural Association, Inc., London (and United Nations Housing Consultant), for the information on Israel; and to the Director of Centro Interamericano de Vivienda y Planeamiento (CINVA) for the details of the Colombia project.

The author also wishes to acknowledge with gratitude permission to quote from *Illustrated English Social History*, by G.M. Trevelyan (Longmans Green and Co. Ltd.); from *London Life in the Eighteenth Century*, by Dorothy M. George (Harper and Row); from *First Essay on Population 1798*, by Thomas Robert Malthus (Facsimile reprint by Macmillan and Co. Ltd.); from *Cities in Evolution*, by Sir Patrick Geddes (Ernest Benn Ltd.); from *Problems of Capital Formation in Underdeveloped Countries*, by Ragnar Nurske (Basil Blackwell); from "Starvation in 1975?", by Richard Spong, quoting Gerard Piel, Publisher of *Scientific American* (*Examiner* [New York], 22 February 1968); from *The Plague,* by Albert Camus (Editions Gallimard: Hamish Hamilton Ltd.); and to summarize pp. 360-64 of *The City is the Frontier*, by Charles Abrams (Harper and Row).

The acknowledgments listed above would be incomplete without the author's expression of appreciation to Mrs. E.T. Hockings for all her valuable help during the laborious and painstaking process of editing.

Contents

List of Illustrations

List of Tables

List of Maps

List of Graphs

"The foci of infection are steadily extending. Judging by the rapidity with which the disease is spreading, it may well, unless we can stop it, kill off half the town . . . That being so, it has small importance whether you call it plague or some other rare kind of fever."

Albert Camus
The Plague

Introduction

Those who have read *The Plague*, that "carefully wrought metaphysical novel",[1] will need no imagination to visualize a city in affliction, to see in their own minds the torment and suffering that follow in the wake of a plague — the horror of the sudden appearance of the buboes, in the groins and glands of the men, women, and children of the town.

One does not *want* to believe that the urban sickness of the "squatter phenomenon" which is afflicting so many of the towns and cities of the developing world today could be as virulent, as insidious, as malignant as the plague, or that its ultimate manifestation in the cities could parallel the final stages of the plague in individuals; but the visible evidence of these vast, rapidly spreading urban squatter colonies indicates that without an energetic programme of action the plague could be back among the cities within the turn of the century. The problem of the urban squatters in the developing nations is a matter of grave concern for the entire civilized world.

Throughout the recorded history of man and his family, the city has been one of the principal instruments for the continued social and economic advancement of society. The

1. So described in the obituary column of *The Times* (London), in 1960, upon the untimely death of the author, Albert Camus.

city is essentially a product of society, "an artificial creation
of society", as Rousseau defines it. As the nature of the city
has stimulated the organizational capacity of the society of
man, so the organizational capacity of man has been able to
mould, shape, and adjust the city to his own convenience.

Over the past millennium, the significance of the city in
many European nations has changed, and particularly so since
the time of the industrial revolution and the colonization era,
when the cities of Europe became the centres of employment
opportunities, attracting and providing employment for skilled
and unskilled workers. Old cities prospered on trade and
commerce, and new cities grew up near the location of the
raw material needed for the industrial expansion. The shift
of population from rural areas to the towns and cities became
noticeable. Furthermore the increase in wealth, and the
capacity for purchasing and importing food more cheaply
from overseas countries, led some of the nations to depend less
and less upon their own rural economy for self-sufficiency in
food. As a result, national investment in the rural areas
diminished progressively until the 1939–1945 conflict caused
the nations to revise considerably their policy on rural-urban
interdependence.

In the developing countries of today, the channelling of
most of the available investment capital into urban industrial
enterprises in the cities in support of the needs of economic
expansion, without a corresponding investment into and protection of the urban nuclei located throughout the agrarian sector
of the country, has caused a growing disproportion between
the living standards of people in the small towns and rural
areas and those enjoyed by the inhabitants of the cities. Food
prices have been deliberately kept low to benefit the urban
dwellers, many of whom are poor, but this has also kept the
income of the rural workers very low. National investment in
the rural areas to provide for the adequate advancement of
resident families has seemingly been neglected, and this has
resulted in an ever increasing social and cultural difference
between rural and urban dwellers.

The consequence of the absence of a properly balanced
rural-urban development programme is an acceleration of the
country-to-city migration trend. But there is a limit to the

amount of in-migration of unskilled and poor families which any city, in either the developed or developing nations, can sustain and still maintain its prescribed average level of living.

In all countries, throughout recent history, this excessive in-migration has resulted in the building up of large colonies of very poorly constructed urban shelters. In the cold climates of European countries in the seventeenth, eighteenth, and nineteenth centuries, and with the appearance on the scene of speculative jerry-builders, the families ceased to be urban squatters and became legitimate tenants, living in badly built urban slums. Climatic conditions in many of the developing nations are tropical or sub-tropical, with the result that the rural-to-urban migrant needs only plaited bamboo strips to construct his shelter — a shelter which, moreover, is perfectly mobile in the sense that, with the help of three or four *compadres*, the hut can be hand-carried from lot to lot, regardless of who legitimately owns the land.

Many of the governments in Europe, through their organizational capacity and empirical adjustment with legislative measures, have been able to control, and, to a high degree, remedy the malady of the massive movement of migrants from the poor rural areas to the cities. This is not the case in the cities of the developing world, where the *rate* of growth of the squatter colonies is such that the squatters, although disassociated members of the urban society today, will assume control of the city before many years elapse, through their constitutional privilege of the vote.

The urban sickness is evidenced at present in the increasing poverty and human deprivation existing in the rapidly expanding towns and cities, in the growing crime rate and juvenile delinquency, in the ever increasing budgetary allocation to prevent cholera epidemics and other malignant diseases from spreading to the remaining population of the city, in "land-grabbing" and disrespect for property rights by a growing number of squatters, in an increasing proportion of illiteracy in the towns, in the mounting social disorder and tension in the cities, in the weakening and breaking down of the administrative discipline of the authorities, in the unsightly human depravity in the midst of, and in sharp contrast with, the affluent established urban society, and in the inadequacy of the essential public services to serve the populace of the cities.

In the cities of more than half the world today, the effective income per head of the city residents, averaged over the total resident population, is becoming less and less each year, and so the effective purchasing power of an increasing proportion of the city residents is diminishing each year, making an ever decreasingly effective demand on the market for industrial consumer commodities. This, in turn, is discouraging the continuous investment of capital in industrial enterprises in these cities, and investment no longer keeps pace with population increase; this trend is only aggravating the urban unemployment problem of such cities and increasing the social tensions.

An increasing proportion of the city population in the afflicted areas can no longer qualify for credit under normal banking procedures, because these people have no security; often, they own their makeshift shack-homes but they occupy the land in defiance of the legitimate owner. They usually have inadequate education, training, or skill to compete in the labour market of the city, and therefore are deprived of the possibility of acquiring regular employment. The opportunities for acquiring work or proper subsistence for the family in the rural areas, should they return, are even less, because very few national development programmes include planned rural resettlement projects which would give the urban squatter, originally from the rural zone, an opportunity to return to the land, and yet be supported by modern-day urban facilities.

The first signs of a metamorphosis of the towns and cities in the developing nations are evident; the change is taking place visibly, as well as being identified in the social and economic forces of the city environment. The visible change reminds one that the houses and buildings, and the physical pattern of the roads, are, as it were, the physical cover or "protective shell" of the "animated city", rather like the carapace of the crustaceans. These animals periodically shed their chitin, and form a new carapace; similarly every twenty, thirty, or forty years, according to the circumstances, cities go through a rebuilding cycle and change their physical cover.

The cities of the developing world are certainly changing the shape and appearance of their "carapace", but if the change continues unguided, unmoulded by the city establishment (and authorities), the final shape of these cities of the future will be very different from the design concepts and dreams of our urban designers of today.

The first signs of the change in the cities indicate that a social readjustment, often self-adjustment, is beginning in many parts of the developing world. The shape and design of the protective shell within which the life of the city can prosper and grow is in considerable doubt because there is no indication yet of the way in which the formation and distribution of capital can be made to match the annual 6 per cent increase in the population of the city. Yet without this capital inflow it is not possible to maintain the existing average urban levels of living.

Albert Camus, in *The Plague*, portrayed the quietly unobtrusive way in which, in times of calamity, the human brotherhood always responds to the suffering of its fellow man, and the way in which volunteer citizen-groups quickly make their appearance and help to carry the burden of order and survival along with established authority. There are many such volunteer groups working busily today amongst the urban slum-squatter colonies in the afflicted towns and cities, making their contribution to the attempt to stem this ever rising tide.

The outward appearance of the malady, the urban squatter colonies, when viewed from the air, from a helicopter, is that of a fungus attached to and growing out from the carapace of the city. Whether, in fact, the dark patches and blotches appearing across the bodies of these cities are really only fungus (which the *Oxford Dictionary* describes as a cryptogamous growth devoid of colour and deriving its sustenance from dead or living organisms), or whether hidden inside the fungin is a more deadly virus, waiting its turn to take its toll like the plague, is something which is not yet known, only feared.

To see in the excessive squalor, filth, and poverty of the urban squatter colonies in the afflicted towns and cities, to see in the human depravity, deprivation, illiteracy, epidemics, and sickness the manifestation of something as malignant as the plague perhaps takes some imagination, but the symptoms of a serious society illness are already evident.

In a city of the Far East, in recent years, the Prefect saw

in the vast urban squatter colonies the equivalent of a plague
breaking out in his city, and, with the concurrence of the District
Court, he prescribed a treatment as if the trouble was indeed
the plague: rapid total clearance and a flaming torch put
to the remnants. The particular area of land was certainly
cleared and made sanitary once more, but the 60,000 people
affected were not extinguished. Just as the plague always
retreats to its lair to wait, the thousands of urban squatters
affected simply slipped into the other already crowded alley-
ways, ghettos, garrets, and other squatter colonies, re-erected
their shacks on the swamp lands, by the side of railway tracks,
on reserved park land, on the river banks, in the many "grottos"
of the cities, causing the existing colonies to stir restlessly and
swell even faster.

The force and power behind the urban squatter problem
is as irresistible, as deceptive to engage, as difficult to control,
as the plague itself. We may perhaps hope to steer or guide it,
but we cannot totally obliterate it, because it is essentially
of human origin.

We know a great deal more about the urban squatters of
the developing world today than we did ten to fifteen years
ago; we know some of their consistent patterns of behaviour,
but not all. We know something of the causes of the malady
which produces this phenomenon, but not nearly enough.
We know some of the treatments to which it may respond, but
the efficacy of these is still unpredictable.

We do know that the urban squatter colonies are swelling
and expanding within many established towns and cities
throughout the Mediterranean area, the Middle East, Asia
and the Far East, and in some African and most Latin American
countries; that they affected the destiny of over 100 million
persons in 1960; and that their number will be likely to treble
by 1980 and continue to swell abnormally thereafter.

A diagnosis of the symptoms indicates that all of the cities
afflicted will undergo, within the foreseeable future, a significant social transformation, and, very likely, a weakening of
the very economic structure on which our civilization has
prospered so far — the city.

The organized society of man is already in a position to
exercise control over much of his urban and living environ-

ment; that is, to a great extent, man's environment is dependent upon his own decisions. If the decisions made in treating both the causes and the effects of the stark and powerful social imbalances of present-day urban life are guided by the needs of humanity, a social readjustment to sustain economic stability can result; but decisions based on primitive concepts of cupidity and the shrewdness and cunning of the animal world, or, on the basis of natural selection, of the survival of the fittest and strongest, will be ineffective against this new manifestation of the plague which will rage unchecked, with the inevitable consequence of death in misery for its victims.

PART ONE

The Urban Squatter Problem

"Scarcity and unemployment on the land have made the cities of the under-developed countries the centres of a worldwide implosion, crowding uncounted millions of people into squatter communities on their perimeters."

Gerard Piel

CHAPTER ONE

The Manifestation of Urban Squatting

Definition of the Urban Squatter

The manifestation of urban squatting is apparent when the rate of in-migration of families from the smaller towns or from rural areas is greater than the rate at which the city can absorb or integrate the families into the existing structure of urban society.

The great majority of the cities of the developing world[1]

---

1. The United Nations publication, *World Population Prospects, As Assessed in 1963* (United Nations, Department of Economic and Social Affairs, Population Studies, No. 41), published in New York in 1966, points out (p. 3) that there is no commonly agreed yardstick by which degrees of development (economic, social, cultural, etc.) are to be measured. However, no other criterion, be it per capita income, urbanization, literacy, industrialization, etc., defines the dichotomy between "developed" and "developing" countries so sharply as the level of human fertility. Where the Gross Reproduction Rate (i.e. G.R.R., the average number of daughters that would be born per woman surviving to the end of her reproductive period in accordance with prevailing age-specific fertility rates) is greater than 2, the country is almost invariably a "developing" one, where the G.R.R. is less than 2, it is almost invariably "developed". The G.R.R. of the developing countries is within the range of 2.2. to 3.5, whereas the G.R.R. for the developed countries is in the range of 1.0 to 1.8.

are already under pressure from the urban squatter problem; they provide a spectacle of masses of poverty-stricken families forming living colonies within, throughout, and around the periphery of established cities.

A distinction is drawn in the subject matter of this book between the "squatter" and the "slum-dweller" of a city. The latter is living in squalor, ably assisted by degenerate and often uninterested landlords, who perpetuate the "skid row" of every city. The slum-dweller pays his rent, and retains his squalor, as a legitimate tenant. Adequate provision exists under the municipal ordinances, and health and sanitation ordinances of most cities of the world today, whereby these "slum ghettos" can be demolished or rehabilitated and proper urban standards of living substituted at the discretion of the local authority. Tragically enough, the programme of urban slum rehabilitation appears to be sadly in arrears.

The urban squatters,[2] the subject of this book, are the illegal occupants of urban land, whether government or private property. They have usually originated from economically depressed rural areas, and over the generations have gravitated from the slum-squatter colony of some miserable small rural town to that of a larger, until those with the highest aspirations for urban living arrive to swell the squatter colonies of the metropolis.

Unable to obtain a piece of land or shelter as legitimate tenants or home owners within the urban society, they use their own initiative; temporary shelters are set up first on any site on which they can enjoy security of tenure for the time being within or on the periphery of the town or city, and, in time, they can exert a moral claim to the site. Their association with the established urban slum is incidental, for they are usually families with an aspiration for self-improvement.

The desire, and the right, of every family to have decent accommodation is not questioned here; but the manner (which is perhaps the only way left open to this ever increasing sub-group of organized urban society) of "staking a claim" and erecting shelters in defiance of all urban standards and regulations, on government and privately owned urban land, is

2. See definition of "squatter": *Shorter Oxford English Dictionary.*

now becoming so common a problem in the great cities of the developing nations of the world — in fact a problem facing the great majority of the United Nations member governments — that as a recognizable phenomenon it can be quantified in international, social, and economic dimensions, and its consequences, if the problem remains unheeded, will be measured in economic loss and the deterioration of our civilization. We will have "lost the peace".[3]

At present, the manner in which 90 per cent of these people live demonstrates not only that their ever mounting numbers are defying established law and authority, but that they are living at levels far below the minimum standards of hygiene and sanitation acceptable for urban living; the disease and sickness in the squatter colonies are a constant reminder of the historical process of city evolution.

The urban squatter colonies in the various cities are known under many names. In Calcutta, Bombay, Delhi, and Karachi, they are known as *bustees, jhoupris, jhuggis*; in Istanbul and Ankara and other cities in Turkey, as *gecekondus*; in Mexican cities, as *jacales* (for provisional squatters); and in Panama City, as *ranchos*. In Brazilian cities, such as Recife, they are called *mocambos*; in São Paulo and Rio de Janeiro, *favelas*; in Porto Alegre, *cortico*. In Tunisian cities, they are termed *gourbivilles*; in Algerian cities, the *casbah*; in Casablanca and other Moroccan cities, *bidonville*; and so on. All the manifestations are similar; all are part of urban squatting. The majority of the families are living in excessively sub-standard conditions, which frequently constitute a menace to the health of the entire city.

[3.] The problem has been recognized in its international content; the United Nations Economic and Social Council in 1967 passed a resolution (1224) and urged member states, in co-operation with the Secretary-General and the United Nations agencies concerned, to undertake practical pilot programmes adapted to the needs of developing countries and directed at the improvement of living conditions in squatter settlements or slums of urban and rural areas, through a simultaneous attack on the social, economic, and physical conditions in such areas, gaining the participation of the citizens concerned and creating, where feasible, institutions and organizations which will promote or support self-improvement.

Fortaleza, Brazil
Typical *mocambos* built by the railway tracks. (Photograph taken 1967.)

THE QUANTITATIVE ASPECTS OF URBAN SQUATTER INCREASE

Unlike the problems of urban expansion which the cities of Europe had to face in the period between the sixteenth and nineteenth centuries, when it is estimated that cities increased in population from 0.6 per cent per annum to 2 per cent per annum,[4] the problem confronting many of the larger cities of the underdeveloped nations today is an annual increase at the rate of 6 per cent, and a visible growth within these cities of urban squatters, in some cases at the rate of 12 per cent per annum.[5]

[4] Kingsley Davis, "The Urbanization of the Human Population", *Scientific American*, September 1965, pp. 41–53.
[5] *Reports of the United Nations Committee on Housing, Building and Planning,* since 1965, and information published by the various local governments.

The urban squatter population of Ankara, capital of Turkey, was reported to be nearly 50 per cent of the population of the city in 1960.[6] In Caracas, Venezuela, in 1964, it was nearly 40 per cent. Cities throughout the Philippines had a squatter problem in 1963 ranging from 20 per cent of the population in Greater Manila to 50 per cent in some of the provincial cities, a problem involving 2,000,000 people.[7] In Djakarta, Indonesia, in 1961, 25 per cent of the urban population registered, approximately 750,000 persons, were urban squatters. In Lima, Peru, in 1965, 45 per cent of the population of the city were squatters, that is, more than a million people.[8] In Rio de Janeiro, Brazil, in 1965, approximately 800,000 people, or 20 per cent of the population of the city, were squatters in *favelas*;[9] in Fortaleza, more than 30 per cent;[10] in Recife, nearly 40 per cent.[11]

A closer study of the social structure of the afflicted cities reveals that there is an increasingly disproportionate number of illiterate, unskilled, nearly unemployable people swelling the urban squatter colonies; this is resulting in a decline in effective purchasing power per head of population, averaged over the whole city community. It can be said that there is an increasingly inequitable distribution of wealth throughout the population of the many afflicted cities, and that an increasing proportion of the population is being denied its full participation in the life and prosperity of the city.

The *World Social Situation*, compiled by the United Nations in 1957, illustrates that in 1800, 2.4 per cent of the world's population lived in towns, whereas by 1960 more than 30 per

6. *Urbanization and Housing Situation in Turkey* (Ministry of Reconstruction and Settlement, Social Research Study No. 2 [Ankara, 1966]).

7. M. Juppenlatz, *Housing the People in the Philippines* (United Nations, Office of Technical Co-operation, TAO/PHIL/14, July 1968).

8. John C. Turner, *Uncontrolled Urban Settlements: Problems and Policies* (Report for United Nations Seminar on Urbanization [Pittsburg, 1966]).

9. See p. 75.

10. Institute of Applied Economic Research, University of Ceará, Fortaleza.

11. Serviços Sociais Contra Mocambos, Recife.

cent of the population were living in urban communities. By the turn of the century, it is expected that nearly 70 per cent of the world's population will be crowded into towns and cities (see Table B).

The United Nations demographers have already established that, over the decade 1950–1960, not only did the population of the world increase by 20 per cent,[12] but the actual increase of approximately 500 million persons over the ten-year period approximately equalled the entire world population of the seventeenth century. Table A (which was compiled by W.F. Wilcox in 1929, and subsequently revised by A.M. Carr-Saunders,[13] and to which the United Nations demographers have now added the 1950 and 1960 world population figures and their predictions for the year 2000) gives some idea of the extraordinary rate of increase of population, and the challenge which lies immediately before the many great cities throughout the world.

Table A. Estimates of world population

Regional zone	Population in millions *(circa)*					
	1650	1750	1850	1950	1960	2000*
AFRICA	100	95	95	206	254	860
AMERICA	13	12	59	329	405	1,143
ASIA	330	479	749	1,386	1,679	4,511
EUROPE (including U.S.S.R.)	100	140	266	576	641	972
OCEANIA	2	2	2	13	16	32
TOTALS	545	728	1,171	2,510	2,995	7,518 (higher variant)

World Population Prospects, as assessed in 1963 (United Nations, Department of Economic and Social Affairs, Population Studies, No. 41 [1966]).

Over the period of time 1960–2000, which is only about half a lifetime, the *urban* population of the world (on present trends) is expected to increase to nearly $4\frac{1}{2}$ times that at present;

12. *World Population Prospects, As Assessed in 1963.*
13. "Estimates of World Population", *Encyclopaedia Britannica* (1961 edn.), XVIII, 232.

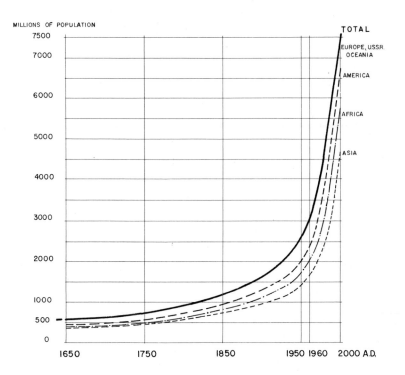

MILLIONS OF POPULATION

Graph for Table A
   Growth trend of world population.

the *urban population* in Africa is expected to increase from 58 million (estimate of 1960) to 294 million; in Asia, from 559 million (1960) to 3,444 million; in Latin America, from 144 million (1960) to 650 million (see Table B for urbanization trends, 1960–2000).

What is significant is the excessively rapid shift from rural to urban areas which is taking place in the less developed regions. A report prepared by the Population Division of the United Nations Bureau of Social Affairs, for the Inter-regional Seminar on Development Policies and Planning in Relation to Urbanization, held in Pittsburg in November 1966, draws attention particularly to this trend (para. 58): "the urban population of the less developed nations might soon comprise the majority of the world's urban population."

Table B. Estimates of increasing urban population in relation to world population, 1960–2000

Regional zone	1960			1980			2000		
	Total	Urban	%	Total	Urban	%	Total	Urban	%
ASIA	1,593.9	288 (559)*	19	2,600	970	37	4,511	3,444	77
EUROPE	427.5	247	58	490	300	61	570	380	67
U.S.S.R.	221.5	100	45	300	145	48	402	200	50
AFRICA	263.0	45 (58)*	17	475	118	24	860	294	34
NORTH AMERICA	264.5	164	62	318	210	66	388	270	69
SOUTH AMERICA	144.7	69 (144)*	48	330	215	65	755	650	86
OCEANIA	14.7	11	70	21	14	66	32	17	53
TOTALS	2,929.8	924	32	4,534	1,972	43	7,518	5,255	70

* See Note to Table C; the figures in brackets represent the estimated urban population for the regions, contained in the estimates prepared by Homer Hoyt (see Note 2 below).

Notes to Table B

1. Estimates of urbanization of world population for 1960 taken from *Scientific American*, September 1965, p. 45; tables contained within the paper by Kingsley Davis, "The Urbanization of the Human Population", from information compiled by the International Population and Urban Research Center, University of California, Berkeley.
2. Percentage of urbanization for the year 2000, for Latin America, Asia, Africa, from estimated urbanization figures quoted in Charles Abrams, *Squatter Settlements: The Problem and Opportunities* (I.M.E., No. 63, Department of Housing and Urban Development [Washington, D.C., 1966]), p. 16, quoting the estimates of Homer Hoyt, in his *Study of International Housing* (Sub-Committee on Housing, Committee on Banking and Currency, U.S. Senate, 88th Congress, 1st Session [March 1963]), p. 17.
3. Estimates of urbanization figures for 1980 by extrapolation.
4. World population for 1980 and 2000 taken from the higher variant, Table A.3.3., *World Population Prospects, as assessed in 1963*, p. 135.

The figures compiled by the United Nations on the trend of urbanization of the less developed nations indicate that the numbers increased from 27 per cent in 1920, to 32 per cent in

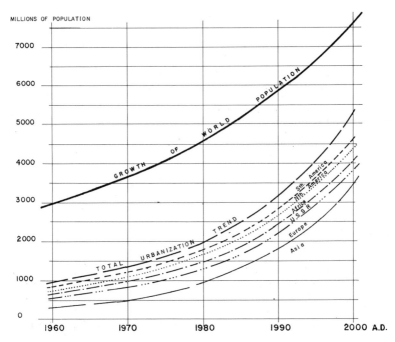

Graph for Table B
Increasing world urbanization trend.

1940, to 42 per cent in 1960; it is estimated that they will increase to 54 per cent of the world total population by 1980.[14]

The results of studies by other authorities on urbanization trends in the less developed nations, such as Dr. Kingsley Davis, International Population and Urban Research Center, Berkeley California, and Homer Hoyt, Urban Land Institute, Washington D.C. (see *World Urbanization* [Technical Bulletin, No. 43, Urban Land Institute]), indicate that (according to the way in which urban and rural communities are defined) the urban population of the less developed nations may well have increased to 66 per cent of world population, the additional

14. *Urbanization; Development Policies and Planning* (United Nations, Department of Economic and Social Affairs, International Social Development Review, No. 1 [New York: United Nations, 1968]), p. 19. (U.N. Sales No. E.68.VI.i.)

Table C. Urbanization trend of less developed regions, 1920–1980

	Population in millions *(circa)*					
	1920	%	1960	%	1980	%
Total population of more developed regions*	672		928		1,129	
Total population of less developed regions +	1,187		2,001		3,405	
TOTAL WORLD POPULATION	1,859		2,929		4,534	
TOTAL URBAN POPULATION	350		924		1,972	
Percentage of urban population to world population		13.5		31.5		43
URBAN POPULATION OF LESS DEVELOPED REGIONS	67.5		402		1,303	
Percentage of urban population of less developed regions to total urban population		27		43.5		66

* More developed regions taken to include: Europe, North America, U.S.S.R., Oceania.
+ Less developed regions taken to include: Asia, Africa, and South America.

Note to Table C and Accompaning Graph

References for United Nations estimates taken from *World Population Prospects. As Assessed in 1963* (United Nations, Department of Economic and Social Affairs, Population Studies, No. 41 [New York: United Nations, 1966]), p. 135, and *Urbanization; Development Policies and Planning* (United Nations, Department of Economic and Social Affairs, International Social Development Review, No. 1 [New York: United Nations, 1968]), pp. 9-19.

The estimates of urbanization trend prepared by the International Population and Urban Research Center, Berkeley, using another index of urbanization (i.e. the proportion of the world's population living in urban places of all sizes), indicated that the urban population in 1960 was more likely 924 million (see Notes to Table B), and the urban population of the less developed regions more likely to be 402 million, increasing (see Table C) to 1,303 million by 1980, not 630 million.

There does not appear to be any universally accepted system for defining and/or measuring urban population in relation to rural population. The census returns for some countries quote the population within the jurisdictional boundary of the local authority

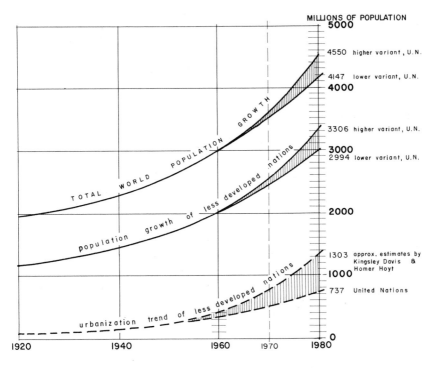

Graph for Table C
Urbanization trend of less developed nations. (For U.N. estimates, see
World Population Prospects, As Assessed in 1963 [United Nations,
1966], Table A3.3/5, p. 135.

of the town, which, in some cases, is so excessively large in area
that much of the population is really rural in nature, character, and
habit. Other census returns have endeavoured to define an urban
area by density of population per hectare, thereby excluding from
the urban population some of the higher-income, lower-density
housing which is far removed from the built-up centre of the town.

There are very few census returns in the world in which the urban
squatters have been enumerated – only dilapidated or sub-standard
housing is recorded.

The urban figures used in Tables B and C can be used only as
a guide to trends of increase in urban living, and not as an accurate
measurement. More accurate recording of urbanization trends will
have to await an internationally agreed definition and an internationally adopted procedure for measuring urban population
growth.

increase presumably being caused by the recent, but significant, movement of population from rural to urban areas (see Table C and accompanying graph).

Mankind has never before been faced with a challenge of such dimensions of human demand and need to test its own organizational capacity to survive. If standards of living are to be maintained only on present levels, which leaves more than 50 per cent of the world at near-starvation point,[15] the expansion of food production, the capacity to industrialize and to accumulate and reinvest capital at a sufficiently fast rate, the provision of the necessary subsistence, work-opportunity, shelter, and clothing will all have to be multiplied several times over.

The problem which is posed by such figures is not only one of increase in numbers, but includes the quantitative aspects of subsistence of supply and demand, caused by the shift from the living standards of presently economically depressed rural areas to those of urban areas. In very general terms, some case studies have revealed the living standard of the average urban squatter to be at least ten times that which he could hope to obtain in the rural zone, and yet his level was still only one-tenth of that of the low-income urban citizen who was already well established.[16] A minimum, but acceptable level of living in urban areas can be defined and quantified under the headings of nutritional intake, shelter, health, education, recreation, and the capacity to save and accrue a surplus. All this is contained within the security of a community environment, which needs to be supported by employment opportunity and urban services such as water supply, sanitation, refuse collection and disposal, power supply, roads, etc. A cost factor for the attainment and maintenance of these levels for

15. The Director-General of the United Nations Food and Agriculture Organization pointed out in the 1967 *Annual Report,* that "birth control and massive food aid have become necessary to save half of the world's population from increasing hunger... the poor crop years of 1965 and 1966 wiped out what little progress the developing nations had made in food production per capita during the past decade".
16. M. Juppenlatz, *Urban Squatter Resettlement, Sapang Palay — A Case Study in the Philippines* (United Nations Report — Restricted).

all of the population, i.e. per capita of the town or city, can be identified.[17]

In order to adjust the differentials in the living standards of the urban squatter with his low-income counterpart (the established member of the urban society), there must exist an additional rate of capital formation for reinvestment into the economy of the town or city to provide for the integration of the peripheral squatters into the social and economic life of the town.

Some indication of the global scale of the problem can be gleaned from Table C, which, though its figures are only approximate, serves to demonstrate the magnitude of the problem, and the extra effort required from organized society to arrest the already deteriorating trend.

If a figure somewhere between 315 million and 402 million is accepted as representing the urban population of the less developed world in 1960, and if, according to calculations based on the percentage relationship of slum-squatters to established urban society for the major cities for which information is available (see p. 15), we assume an average of 30 per cent of the urban population of the less developed nations to be slum-squatters, then there would have been approximately 100 million such urban slum-squatters in the less developed nations in 1960. These people have little direct earning capacity, little opportunity to raise their average level of productivity, low purchasing power, and altogether make a negligible contribution to the economic progress, or treasury, of the town.

On the assumption that a universal policy could be adopted and implemented to raise the living standards of these squatters and integrate them into the urban society by an investment programme — a programme aimed at upgrading their human resources by equipping them with a trade or skill to make possible their assimilation into the employment structure of the city, and supported by a similar investment in the sphere of urban services and facilities such as additional school places,

17. Jan Drewnowski, *Social and Economic Factors in Development: Introductory Considerations on Their Meaning, Measurement and Interdependence* (United Nations Research Institute for Social Development, Report No. 3 [Geneva, 1966]).

hospital beds, extension of piped water supply, housing programmes, etc. — and assuming that this urban integration could
be achieved at a total urban investment rate equivalent to
US$1000 per head, the total investment required to deal with
the backlog of 1960 would equal US$100,000 million *(circa)*.
This plan, programmed over a period of twenty years, to
assimilate the squatter dwellers of 1960, would mean the
equivalent of US$5,000 million invested throughout the urban
centres of the entire underdeveloped world annually. This is
by no means beyond the financial resources of the countries,
the great majority of which are member nations of the United
Nations. The value of the increase in the gross capital formation
of the town or city within such a *squatter* urbanization programme would more than recompense the investment, and
this would provide for continuity of advancement for the
benefit of future generations as well.

However, the information available on trends of urban
population increase reveals that within the same twenty-year
period the total urban population of the *less developed nations*
could increase to 1,300 million. Even if the problem were held
in its present status by a programme of action dealing with the
backlog of squatters in 1960, a high proportion of the increased
urban population would have been derived from the in-
migration of poverty-stricken former rural dwellers, increasing
probably by as much as 5–10 per cent per annum.

A global investment programme for the urbanization of
squatters would require the equivalent of US$5,000 million
in the initial years, increasing annually thereafter at a geometric
rate to match the continuing increase of the urban squatters,
i.e. increasing by approximately 5–10 per cent per annum.

Though the statistical returns of the "national accounts"
for most of the countries indicate an improvement in their
Gross National Product every year of approximately 5 per
cent,[18] and though, in total, the returns indicate (on a national
average) an improvement of productivity per capita, this is
often derived more from the increased productive efficiency

18. There is actually a considerable fluctuation in the value of
    Gross National Product of the various developing nations —
    between 3 and 7 per cent over a period of years; the average
    of 5 per cent G.N.P. is a generalization only.

of the established industrial enterprises through mechanization than from an actual increase in the productivity of the average individual. Not all of the urban population of these countries are benefiting directly from the increase in national wealth.

THE EVER WIDENING CYCLE OF POVERTY

The questions must inevitably be raised whether the social contract of the people with their government in the under-developed nations is adequate, whether the constitutional framework and administrative, organizational, and executive capacity of such governments are equal to the task before them, and finally whether the people themselves have the capacity to produce the food and create the wealth required to sustain industrial support for the improving levels of living. The cycle of poverty, once begun, is a vicious cycle which is difficult to break, without external support and assistance from the established society.

Just as there exists in the natural environment of weather a perpetually changing pattern of high and low pressure systems, so there exist in the social environment cyclical changes in the equilibrium of high and low patterns of society.

Just as an imbalance or an excessive differential in the weather pressure systems causes violent storms, typhoons, tornadoes, or cyclones, so excessive differentials in social pressures cause revolutions, wars, etc.

Thomas Malthus[19] hypothesized that the perfectibility of society, its capacity to reach a state where every man shall be equal, was an unattainable dream because of the incontrovertible truth that population will continue to grow in a geometric ratio, whilst subsistence can be provided only at an arithmetic ratio of increase, thereby retaining a large segment of the population in a perpetual state of poverty.

Poverty, a recognizable and definable low pressure system of our society, is also recognized as being an age-old vicious

19. Thomas Robert Malthus, *First Essay on Population, 1798* (A reprint in facsimile of *An Essay on the Principle of Population As It Affects the Future Improvement of Society* [1798]; London: Macmillan, 1966), chapter 2.

cycle in itself. Dr. Ragnar Nurske[20] describes it as "a circular constellation of forces tending to act and react upon one another in such a way as to keep a poor country in a state of poverty".

More than 160 years after Malthus wrote his *Essay on the Principle of Population, As It Affects the Future Improvement of Society*, nearly half the world's population is suffering from malnutrition. It is particularly prevalent in all of the urban slum-squatter colonies in the less developed nations.

Dr. Andomaro Guevara estimates that in Latin America alone 600,000 children die every year from starvation, whilst a further 37 per cent of the population is suffering from malnutrition.

> Large numbers of children in the hemisphere survive despite the poor food supply, but they join the ranks of deteriorated citizenship.[21]

The situation is estimated to be far worse on the Asian mainland. Already India has begun mass sterilization; 3.5 million have undergone the operation, and this alone is calculated to prevent the birth of a further 10 million over the next ten years. The population of India, 515 million, is estimated to be increasing at the rate of 13 million a year.[22]

An example of the working of a circular constellation of poverty is demonstrated within the context of malnutrition. The poor squatter is underfed; being underfed, his health, energy, and morale are weakened considerably, and his working capacity thereby greatly reduced. Because his personal productivity is so low, he is retained in a state of poverty and in this state he is unable to raise the money necessary to buy enough food for himself or his family. And so the family stays at near-starvation level, with no means of escape or elevation to anything better.

In the case of poorer, less developed countries, the low real

20. Ragnar Nurske, *Problems of Capital Formation in Underdeveloped Countries* (New York: Oxford University Press, 1964), chapter 1.
21. Dr. A. Guevara, Director of the National Child Welfare Institute, Address to the Seminar on Nutrition and Child Feeding, Mexico City, March 1968.
22. Csripati Chandrasekhar, Minister for Family Planning, Release of statement to Council of State, India, March 1968.

income is a reflection of low productivity, to which the lack of capital is often a significant contributory cause. This has usually resulted from, and can often be attributed to, the small capacity of the country to save; and so the cycle of poverty continues.

Dr. Nurske describes with clarity that the *accumulation* of capital, which provides the means of continuous economic growth, is dependent upon the capacity of the country to *save*, whereas the *demand* for capital depends upon incentives which are available throughout the many investment sectors of the national economy.

> On the demand side, the inducement to invest may be low because of the small buying power of the people, which is due to their small real income, which again is due to low productivity. The low level of productivity, however, is a result of the small amount of capital used in production, which, in its turn, may be caused at least partly by the small inducement to invest.[23]

The low level of real income, reflecting low productivity, is a point that is common to both circles.

The capacity of a nation to save is also linked inextricably with its tendency to spend, and this involves the direction, or the various segments of the economic life of the country, into which the spending is channelled.

John Maynard Keynes, in his *General Theory of Employment, Interest and Money*,[24] demonstrated that the rate of spending by either the public or the private sector is never a self-correcting behaviour; it is cumulative. He recommended that, in the interests of self-preservation, and in order to avoid the crippling economic fluctuations and perpetual devaluation which characterized the cycle of economic trends in Europe throughout the nineteenth and early twentieth centuries, the State needs to acquire a strong influence over the flow and direction of the capital of the country.

The consequences of the combination of such an unguided behavioural trend with the effects of excessive migration from rural areas into a city, to a point of saturation where the productive capacity per head, on total average, is so weakened that the total purchasing power of the inhabitants

23. Nurske, *op. cit.*
24. New York: Harcourt, Brace and World, 1936.

does not increase (despite an annual 6 per cent increase of population), can be seen in a case study of Rio de Janeiro in 1967.

The metropolitan area of the City of Rio de Janeiro, with a population of 4.4 million persons in 1960, actually spreads over an area embracing two States. At the time of the case study, 3.2 million persons in the City of Rio de Janeiro were in the State of Guanabara, whilst the remainder, 1.2 million, were resident in the adjoining State of Rio de Janeiro, resident mostly in the City of Niterói.

The results of the case study were published in the daily press on 25 July 1967,[25] and revealed that for the ten-year period, 1949–1958, the value of product of the State of Guanabara, which is, for the most part, the City of Rio de Janeiro, rose *annually* by 4 per cent (on average); the value of product showed *no* increase annually over the period 1959–1963, and, from that time on, began to show a decline — of 1.5 per cent in 1964, and, by the end of 1965, of 8.5 per cent. In total, over the period 1961–1964, the value of product of the city-state is reported to have dropped by 16 per cent whilst the per capita income dropped 24 per cent; yet population had increased by 24 per cent.

With the indication that the per capita purchasing power of these cities is declining (or alternatively, that the total annual market for products, based on the purchasing power of the inhabitants of the city, is not increasing annually at a rate commensurate with the actual increase of population), investors and entrepreneurs in such cities are inclined to limit their investment in the establishment of new industrial and consumer factories to the known or predictable market which is available. The net result is that, in the laissez-faire economic system of many of the developing countries, industrial employment opportunities are not being created in the cities in any way commensurate with increasing labour needs. It is the cities in themselves that are the centres of attraction, a situation quite different from that which caused the movement to the cities in nineteenth-century Europe, when labour moved to centres of industry, thereby establishing a new pattern of

25. *Correio da Manhã*, 25 July 1967.

urban settlement throughout the land — one based on the location of resources for industrialization.

In the developing nations, with the available market being met as a result of the improved industrial efficiency which followed on mechanization and with the average per capita purchasing power diminishing, much of the available investment capital (and it is, for the most part, limited) is being diverted to quick capital formation investments. Among these is the age-old system of urban land speculation which, with its speculative inflationary trend, makes urban land totally unavailable to the poor, on any open negotiations. An after-effect of this form of inflationary investment is that the city is being deprived of the investment capital vitally needed for its balanced development and for the extension of an industrialization of productive employment programme. The unemployment problem, both within the city and in total, is being aggravated, and is setting in motion an adverse economic trend for the city as a whole, which cumulatively will be reflected in an adverse trend for (or at least, a retardation of) the entire national economy.

The problem of the cycles of poverty, then, is contained within the problem and cycles of economic growth. Irrespective of the basic political, administrative, or social evolutionary process which prevails in any one country at any one time, economic growth can be said to be concerned with the accumulation of capital at a geometric rate to match both the increasing rate of population and the rising level of living, both urban and rural.

In European and North American countries, economic growth has been achieved to a considerable extent by the application of the scientific method, along with a gradual acceptance by the State of a strong influence over the direction of the capital flow of the nation. It is seemingly time for the introduction of the scientific method in the total planning processes of the rural-to-urban interdependence factors of the less developed nations.

THE FALLACY OF URBAN LAND HUNGER

Compounding the squatter problem in the cities of underdeveloped countries is the problem of land speculation in the cities, and the excessively inflationary spiral of urban land prices. This is particularly prevalent in nations which have inherited the old colonial Spanish Title systems of land tenure.

In some of the major metropolises of the *developed* countries, certain forms of taxation on land, and control of land use, in addition to an effective administrative system for urban planning and development, encouraging the redistribution and density of population, have been used effectively to curb runaway inflation in the price of urban land.

In many of the less developed countries, in the absence of any urbanization programme, subdivided land, with roads partially constructed (some with concrete kerbs), but with no water supply, no main drainage system for surface run-off, no sewerage system, and no transport system to the city or places of employment, is found far removed from the built-up sections of the city, anticipating a demand within a few years by the very pressure of population in the cities. The land, or lots, of these estates are usually priced at fully developed urban land value, which normally presumes the existence of schools, marketing and recreational facilities, public utility services, etc. Yet these facilities do not exist. This land is priced far beyond the financial capacity of more than 90 per cent of the rural in-migrants to the city.

Urban land prices have been increasing in most of the less developed nations of the world during the past decade; they have increased so far above the general price levels that this has now become a serious obstacle to further urban progress. In the post-war era, owners of capital in a great many cities throughout the world found that urban real estate was a most lucrative investment, providing higher returns over shorter periods than almost any other avenue of investment; not only are these circumstances persisting, but prices are becoming extravagant in the extreme in the many cities of the developing nations, as the pressure of population continues to build up.

The extent to which the authorities of some of the developing nations are able to regulate land values is limited, particularly when their "democratic constitutions" protect the rights of all private land ownership and where the concept of uncon-trolled "profit motive" is still regarded as the stimulus for all economic progress; this poses a dilemma as to exactly how the regulation of land values can be achieved, for the voting public is involved, and this means the members of the legislature itself.

Urban land values have appreciated mostly through improvements to the local environment at public expense. The pressure of population on urban land, and the resulting demand for urban land (developed or underdeveloped), have in turn generated the large element of potential development value, resulting in the excessively inflated values. It would not appear unreasonable for the local authorities to increase the tax on the profit of the land transactions (i.e. the difference between the "assessed value" and the "sale value"), and for the government to use the proceeds to provide the basic infrastructure, to acquire more land on which some of the squatter families could be re-accommodated within their meagre incomes, and also on which the local authority could proceed with the construction of low-cost public housing projects.

Part of the programme should be to assimilate the urban squatters, who have been denied their proper urban citizenship by the very inflationary trend of land values, into the established urban scene, as has been undertaken in Hong Kong and Singapore. As historical experience has shown, there is every justification for local authorities in the developing countries to exert a greater fiscal and social control over the flow of capital, and now, also, over the development and control of urban land.

There is no actual shortage of land for urban use; the amount of land utilized for urban purposes is often less than 1 per cent of the total land of the country, and rarely is the percentage of urban land higher than 5 per cent, even in the most densely populated countries. The current situation does, however, reveal the highly concentrated centres of wealth throughout the country, and therefore, the magnets of attraction for the bulk of the population. There is no shortage of land in any of the developing nations, for the most densely populated countries are not to be found in Africa, or the Americas, or Asia, where the densities are 8, 9, and 60 persons respectively per square kilometre, but in the Netherlands, in Europe, where the density is 350 per square kilometre.[26]

26. Charles Abrams, *Squatter Settlements: The Problem and Opportunities* (I.M.E., No. 63, Department of Housing and Urban Development [Washington D.C., 1966]).

Singapore
  Extension of the new town concept to include industrial estate and
  high-density housing. (Photograph taken 1962.)

Many cities of the developing world today are engaged in
the drawing up of plans for the orderly extension of public
health services and the expansion of community facilities
throughout and around urban centres.

However, along with the drawing up of plans to add to
the convenience and comfort of the city residents, has come
the realization that the earning capacity of migrants from the
rural areas, who are annually swelling the numbers in the
squatter colonies of the cities, is so low, through their lack of
skill and training, that the way is not yet clear for them to
undertake any normal urban financial commitment; they do
not qualify for loans under present banking and loan conditions,
and they have no means with which to purchase urban land,
and certainly not at its presently inflated value. This means
that they pay no taxes to the local authority, and make no

contribution towards amortizing the loans required for providing essential public services to peripheral urban development. The result is that many city authorities do not provide such services to the squatter colonies, but leave the problem almost unheeded.

URBAN SQUATTING — A CREEPING PARALYSIS OR A SOCIAL TRANSFORMATION

As the squatters continue to increase their numbers in many cities throughout the world, their influence in the political structure of each local government increases proportionally. The urban squatter problem in many cities is now entering the "power political" phase; by the constitutional voting rights of the people, these cities will soon be theirs to command.

The first-generation urban squatter families invariably have inadequate education, training, or skill to compete in the labour market of the city, and are therefore unable to acquire regular employment. The opportunities for acquiring work or proper subsistence, should these families choose to return to the rural areas, are even less, because there are very few national development programmes which include planned rural settlement for the poor and unskilled. In fact, there appear to be few national development programmes geared towards planned redistribution of population according to the land and settlement resources of the country, and aimed at self-sufficiency in the matter of food, clothing, and shelter within prescribed minimum levels of living.

The problem of squatting is the same in all the underdeveloped countries, ranging from emergent nations, such as Papua, New Guinea, to more advanced nations such as Brazil. With the spirit of progress which prevails throughout the world of today, brought about by advances in communication, people are endeavouring to equalize the levels of urban living as quickly as possible. In effect, what is required is an acceleration of the urban social evolutionary process. Coupled with this process is the necessity to accelerate the process of generating wealth, which in itself is a highly sensitive undertaking, demanding a high degree of academic skill in trade, finance, and banking, in addition to a well-framed administrative system. In the case of Papua, New Guinea, there is the delicate transformation of former hill-tribe, coastal, or rural dwellers into urban dwellers, requiring an action programme by the administrators of the territory to provide for the total reorientation of their mentality towards, and a recognition of their obligations in, established urban society.[27]

N.D.Oram stresses that poverty in itself is not the only major cause of undesirable and insanitary living conditions in the less developed nations, and he questions whether the building ordinances, by-laws, and regulations are not unrealistic, considering the circumstances of the towns, being in fact written only for the high standards desired for the few; whether, in East African towns or in New Guinea, the urban areas in these emergent nations usually included a large section inhabited by migrant foreigners, such as the administrators and trade and commercial officials or representatives, which remained very much a separate enclave and could be termed the high-grade area, whilst the low-grade areas were inhabited by the indigenous people, the great majority of whom were in-migrants from the rural hinterland, or from smaller towns.

The colonies of the latter were invariably extended considerably because of family or kinship ties. The same kinship pattern with the in-migrants to the cities can be found in the squatter colonies throughout the Philippines, India, and the Latin American nations, and is known as the "extended family" system; as one member of the family gains employment or a status in the town, other members of the family join him to share some of the advancement.

The occupants of the high-grade areas can afford to subscribe to the costs of urban "furniture and equipment", such as paved roads, drains, etc., public transport, public services and facilities such as power and water supply, refuse collection and disposal, street cleaning, etc. For their own comfort and convenience, such are adequately provided, but, as was said above, occupants of low-grade areas cannot make any financial contribution to the amortization of the municipal loans necessary for the extension of public services, and so such facilities are not provided by the local authorities.

[27]. N. D. Oram, "Health, Housing and Urban Development", *Architecture in Australia,* November 1966, p. 98 (Reprint from the *Papua and New Guinea Medical Journal,* September 1965).

Oram describes how there exist throughout the urban squatter colonies of the indigenous population in Port Moresby the same sickness factors as are found in all the squatter colonies throughout Asia; malnutrition, delinquency, mental disorders, and increasing venereal disease, all of which can be attributed to the physical and social environment of the squatter colonies.

It would appear that little consideration has yet been given by the authorities to the human force which is being generated in the cramped, sordid, unhygienic, peripheral squatter colonies, and the day when that growing human force will seek a better adjustment of social levels in the cities.

Endeavouring to limit this inflow of human waves into the cities, as some South African authorities[28] tried to do, has not succeeded, for the squatters retain themselves always just outside of the jurisdictional area of the local authority, reflecting the historical experience of the towns and cities of Britain in the eighteenth century. Limiting the influence of these squatter dwellers in local government by denying them the right to vote on their residency status, as was tried in some Latin American countries, was only very temporary in its effectiveness.

Throughout the world, the majority of squatter colonies, which range in size from 8 to 80,000 persons in each, are without essential public services; very few colonies have a proper piped water supply to each house; there are rarely any sewer connections, or adequate provision made for sanitation; there are few or no proper land storm-water drainage systems; and there is no organized system for refuse collection and disposal, which means that filthy mounds of garbage are left to breed disease and foster sickness among the squatter families, and represent a continual threat of outbreak of disease throughout the rest of the city.

There are, of course, minimal standards of urban sanitation and hygiene which should be adopted for these peripheral colonies, and, with the introduction of some community self-help action through an educational programme, the burden of some of the cost of refuse collection, sanitation (for instance, pit latrines), land drainage, etc., can be undertaken by the

28. *Ibid.*

people of the community themselves. Roadways can be aligned and constructed and houses re-erected preparatory to the transfer of the title to and the ultimate ownership of the land by the former squatter, within a physical development undertaking. Such an approach at integrating the squatters requires the direct participation of and guidance from the local authority. The labour for the actual construction of the roads can be marshalled from the labour pool of the slum-squatter colonies themselves, with a subsistence payment being made in both food and cash.

The causes, motivation, aspirations, and conditions of squatters will be dealt with at some length in the case studies in this paper, but it should be recognized that the urban squatters have become, for the most part, organized sub-societies within the established urban society. There is now emerging a recognizable hegemony, with its own hierarchical pattern among most of the squatter colonies, which is now capable of negotiating politically with the established authority and society. Not all the squatters are living in squalor; in some countries, such as the Philippines, it is estimated that 10–15 per cent are inveterate speculators who have no intention of waiting, and who in fact can well afford not to wait (in discomfort) for the day when their illegal possession of the land on which they are situated will ultimately be legalized by the political process. It has been demonstrated throughout history that with sufficient numbers exerting a moral claim on land the action of legalizing the transfer of ownership is an inevitable consequence.

The prevailing circumstances in so many cities today in the less developed nations herald the beginning of a creeping paralysis; whether this trend can be averted to one of a social transformation through changes in the patterns of political leadership and philosophy, in the distribution and control of wealth in the city and throughout the land, and in the trends of economic growth, is the real issue facing humanity in the immediate future.

CHAPTER TWO

Several Methods of Approaching the Problem

The Phenomenon Is Constant – The Treatment Is Not

Over the years of history, most cities have grown up with an identifiable character of their own. This was particularly so, until the industrialization process began to attract waves of migrants from the rural areas to the peripheries of the towns and cities in search of employment and higher wages. For all this, a town or city, in total expression, can be considered as reflecting the multiple character of the individuals resident in the community, and therefore as reflecting their composite function, needs, and aspirations.

The health, sicknesses, ailments, social balances and imbalances of the city as a whole can all be measured, diagnosed, and treated within the disciplines, laws, and rules governing the health and happiness of the individual. The disciplines and laws become proportionally more complex with the increase of population, with the many variables associated with the circulatory processes (necessary for the life of the city), the variable and complex social strata and hierarchy of allegiances, and the forces of economic motivation.

The "rash" now appearing across many of the townscapes of the modern cities in the developing world, caused by the growing urban squatter colonies, and spreading with such rapidity throughout these cities (until it will soon cover more than half their area), needs to be diagnosed, and the *cause* of the "rash" treated as well as the *effect*.

There are several examples in countries throughout the world, where the authorities simply cleared specific squatter colonies of their inhabitants, with no concern for the destiny of the displaced families except that they should be anywhere but on that particular site. The benefit to the health and economy of the city was that the particular site was cleared; on the debit side, the displaced families simply re-established themselves on other vacant sites in the city, government-owned or privately owned, at the same time suffering some social dislocation and becoming, if anything, a little more defiant towards the local authority.

There are, however, some examples where national and local government have joined forces to treat the problem in its totality and have viewed the urban squatter problem as one originating from the human needs of these people for shelter, employment, and communal and social services; some governments are well advanced in the formulation of national urbanization programmes, in which the programme of resettlement, rehousing, and relocation of urban squatters is an integral part of the overall programme. Some examples are to be found in the Middle East, Asia, and Brazil.

Some governments are exploring the possibility, within the provisions of their constitutions, of rehabilitating the squatter families on the sites on which they are situated, with a view to integrating the families into normal urban life and citizenry, and dealing with the land tenure problem separately. Several examples are to be found in Latin America.

There are also some examples of governments providing programmes for the redistribution of some of the urban squatters into new agrarian communities within a regional development concept. Malaya has such a programme, and there are other programmes, such as that devised by the Government of Brazil for establishing agro-industrial villages throughout the "pioneer fringes" of the State as an alternative destination for the rural migrant.

Whether to encourage the relocation of many of the urban squatter families into new communities outside the city, whether to provide adult vocational education or training

courses in the squatter colonies to upgrade the earning capacity
of the inhabitants, whether to accommodate them in social
housing projects and provide training courses for their integration into normal city life — all these are questions which
are being asked daily by government policy-makers all around
the world, and any of these plans would involve some segment
of the public purse. Without a proper scientific diagnosis,
decisions are being made which still leave many human and
economic problems in their wake. Other governments, working
on the basis of an integrated humanization and urbanization
programme, have at least been able to stem the rising tide.

Of the several action programmes which have been adopted
throughout the world, the following have been included
because, adopted singly or in combination to suit specific local
conditions, each has its place if a universal programme is to
be drawn up, aimed at finally bringing about the social readjustment of the urban squatter in this rapidly urbanizing world.

PLANNED NATIONAL DEVELOPMENT — INTEGRATION OF URBAN
IN-MIGRANTS

Dr. Otto Koenigsberger[1] propounds the thesis that where
the moral and social philosophy of the established authority
provides three basic needs for the in-migrants on a programmed
basis, namely work, shelter, and a welcome into the community,
the in-migrants can become a blessing to the community as a
whole, and not a liability. A positive investment programme is
needed by the authorities to reduce the time-lag between the
time of arrival of the newcomers, and the time when they
will begin to pay taxes to the community treasury. By doing

1. Observations by Dr. O. Koenigsberger, Head of the Department
of Tropical Studies, Architectural Association, Inc., London,
and United Nations Housing Consultant, during a lecture tour
of Brazil, 1968. Full details of the migrant assimilation programme, and the land settlement and urbanization programme
of Israel can be obtained from the Government of Israel; the
programme has been treated on a "laboratory basis", and all
facets of the programme, success, modification, etc. have been
well documented and recorded.

this, the established authorities provide for the early assimilation of the newcomers into the community, and eliminate the tendency to "squat". The programme of action devised by the Government of Israel is used to illustrate this particular approach.

In 1962, when the total population of Israel was some 2,000,000 persons, the government anticipated, and in previous years had been accommodating, an inflow of 100,000 migrants a year into the cities and villages. The government recognized the importance of having a total land settlement plan interdependent with a national urbanization programme, and consciously programmed the reception, relocation, housing, and early integration of the families into their local society, whether urban or rural.

Where possible, even before the arrival of the family into the country, the in-migrant was classified by his or her aptitude and/or preferences for agrarian pursuits or assimilation into urban life. Once the decision was made, the in-migrant families were provided with training, along with a loan, and a house or apartment ready for occupancy, and complete with essential furniture, cooking equipment, and a supply of food.

If the in-migrant had an aptitude for a trade or skill suited to urban living, he was reckoned to be in a position to make his contribution to costs of urban administration and services and to be able to commence to pay taxes and the repayment of the loan within six months of settling into his new house.

If the family elected an agrarian activity, they were not expected to begin repayments earlier than eighteen months after taking up their job.

The programme of assimilating the newcomers was treated as a strictly commercial operation; the loan which the newcomer received on arrival included the cost of his orientation and resettlement; the programme of in-migration was coupled with a programme of planned investment by the central bank, which was geared to the creation of so many extra places of employment each year to sustain productivity.

The programme for absorbing the families (many of whom had come from a variety of countries and had been extremely poor in their former abodes) is part of a national urbanization programme, which is related directly with a programme of planned land development. Integrated within their programme is a national housing programme, of which the government is responsible for approximately 66 per cent, while the remainder is undertaken by the private sector.

Construction of houses has been at the rate of 16 dwellings per 1,000 population per annum, a rate of home construction which is amongst the highest in the world. The houses were constructed within an urban physical, social, and economic plan, sometimes in complete new towns, planned for populations ranging from 40,000 to 100,000 persons. Most of these towns were built up of neighbourhood or social planning units of 5,000 to 10,000 persons.[2]

Planned and programmed assimilation of all the in-migrants into a viable economic expansion programme, and planned labour and settlement distribution, have resulted in a rapid transition of the in-migrants from their former state of poverty to one of a measurable productivity factor per head; all of this is accumulating wealth for the nation, thereby making possible a continuation of the programme of raising the living standards of all those existing now, and also of those who will follow in the next decades.

What is so important is that the authorities recognized the danger of permitting tens of thousands of families merely to transfer from the subsistence economy of their former rural abodes to a subsistence economy in the urban centres; a positive investment programme was prescribed by which the families, after a period of training and orientation, became established tax-paying citizens — i.e., within six to eighteen months of their arrival.

Assimilation Through Urban Redevelopment Programmes

In examining a squatter integration programme for a city (in this case, New Delhi is taken as an example), the background of the origin of the city, and its evolution through time is of significance, since the urban squatter problem must have originated at some point of time in the history of the city, and

2. Joan Ash, "Planning and Housing for Immigrants in Israel", *Ekistics,* XXIII, No. 135 (February 1967), 83.

originated from a specific set of economic circumstances surrounding the city at that time. This being the case, an assessment of the issues involved should pave the way for a more sympathetic policy towards, and subsequent treatment of, the urban slum-squatter problem.

For this reason, a very brief historical background of the city of New Delhi is included, to provide a better perspective of the programme which has been adopted.

(a) *The emergence of Delhi — The city*

The urban squatter problem of Delhi in 1963 was no less in its dimension than those of Hong Kong, Manila, Rio de Janeiro, and several other great cities of the world, and the origin of its squatting problem lies in the same root causes, those of constitutional change and socio-political upheaval throughout the land, accompanied by a gravitational movement of under-privileged rural families to the employment opportunities in the centres of wealth.

The rural-to-urban migrations became noticeable during the 1939–1945 war, when large military establishments were located near the major cities, such as Delhi, providing a great deal of additional employment. With the cessation of inter-national hostilities came independence, partitioning, and much confusion, chaos, and bloodshed. The partition agreements between India and Pakistan necessitated the sudden social readjustment of millions of people.

The rural-urban balance of the nation was totally disrupted — refuge in the city became the only hope for those not tied to the land.

Planned and programmed development was the policy of the newly independent government, and from the outset the significance of planned urban development within its regional economic context was recognized as an essential function of the government. An urbanization programme was adopted for Delhi, in which provision was made for both the clearance of slum areas and the accommodation of the ever increasing numbers of squatter families.

The authorities of Delhi have an advantage in conceiving a programme of growth and development for the city of the future, for there is a wealth of experience of urban growth, decay, and development on which they can call from the very history of the city itself.

Though no doubt cities existed on the present site of Delhi before the eleventh century A.D., it is from that time, when Anang Pal, the Rajput Chief of the Hindu Toimara Clan, built the first Red Fort (on the site known today as Qutb Minar and known then as Indraprastha), that history recognizes Delhi. The various cities built on or around the present site have been subjugated, built, demolished, and rebuilt over the centuries, with the coming of the Muhammadans in their separate phases.

Over the period 1638–1658, Shah Jahan built the Red Fort of Delhi and the great wall surrounding Shahjahanabad; within this wall and close by the Red Fort, over the period 1630–1656, there was built Jama Masjid, often referred to as the greatest mosque of all. Around the mosque soon grew the market and the bazaar, in their day amongst the most exotic on the caravan routes of the East.

With the usual compactness of oriental markets (frontages of 12–15 feet), the foundations were laid for a congested mixed land usage (the standard practice in most cities) of commercial, light industrial, and residential, often in vertical stratification, as well as horizontal. The families and traders of the day looked on the congestion as something which provided them with security, and also as a factor which attracted intensified commercial and trade activity.

Over the centuries, as a result of the strong brotherhood ties that exist among the various provincial, religious, and ethnic groups, relatives or "brothers" from the rural areas have come to the city to share both accommodation and opportunities for gaining wealth with their established relatives.[3]

As the hospitality of the city-dweller provided accommodation for more and more of his provincial "family", so the density of families living together became greater and greater, and the levels and standards of environmental sanitation, drainage and sewerage disposal, refuse disposal, and standards of light and air about the building diminished proportionally.

[3.] The same "blood" or loyalty affiliations found in Asian squatter colonies are to be found also throughout all the Latin American countries, or any of the former Spanish colonies.

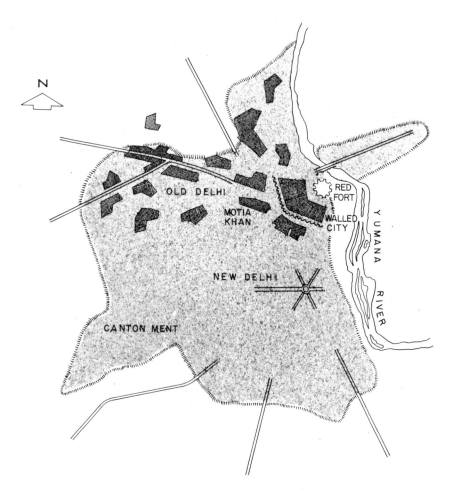

Delhi, India
  Urban slum-squatter colonies (1966).

Meanwhile, the British East India Company, incorporated by Queen Elizabeth I under royal charter in December 1600 and entitled "The Governor and Company of Merchants, trading in the East Indies", was proving itself to be a most profitable trading enterprise. In 1612, it was converted into a joint-stock company, and under the five charters granted by

King Charles II grew into one of the great chartered companies, with extensive privileges, concessions, and powers to negotiate control over territory.

After Robert Clive's victory at Plassey (Palasi) in 1757, which made the company a ruling power in India, the British Government decided that it was necessary to exercise some control over the territories gained by the company. Pitt's India Bill of 1784 created a Board of Control, as a department of the British Government, authorized to exercise political, military, and financial superintendence over British possessions in India. This continued until Earl Grey's act of 1833, which ended monopoly of the tea trade with China and caused the company to cease to be a trading concern, and exercise an administrative function only. The result proved to be unsatisfactory, and, with the Indian Mutiny in 1857, the British Government transferred the administration of India to the Crown.

In 1911 the authorities planned and built a new centre of administration for India, New Delhi, adjacent to, but disassociated from, the old city. The old city, apart from ancient historical monuments, rapidly began to show signs of neglect and decay, physically, socially, and economically. However, with the introduction of industrial and commercial processes during the nineteenth century, many changes in the urban social stratification had taken place, and the old city still continued to attract many from the rural areas. These migrants were so totally unequipped for the urban pattern of living, and their numbers increased so greatly compared with the established urban society, that

> the urban social structure (of Old Delhi) changed during the late nineteenth century, and early twentieth century, from a coherent body to a heterogeneous group of diversified elements and interest . . . the result was serious disorder and unplanned concentration of peoples . . . there was much congestion, functional obsolescence, ugliness, poor housing, filthy *katras* and *bustis*, with all round blight and decay, throughout the old city.[4]

As the metropolis expanded outside the walled city during the nineteenth century, so the disorderly spread of settlement

4. *The Draft Master Plan of Delhi* (Delhi Development Authority, 1966), Vol. I, chapter 9.

extended itself even further, and when New Delhi was declared capital of India in 1912 the ex-rural metropolitan population intensified. The population of the combined New and Old Delhi rose from 247,000 in 1921 to 1,440,000 in 1951, and to 2,660,000 in 1961 — a rate of growth of 75 per cent over the decade 1941–1951, and of 51.4 per cent between 1951 and 1961. The authorities have attributed this sustained high rate of increase to continued unemployment in the surrounding rural areas, and to the intensified economic activity of the metropolis during the 1941–1945 war years.[5] Having once migrated to the cities, the families rarely return to their rural homes, for even though they may be unemployed in the city, there is still less for them to return to in the rural provincial areas.

(b) *Urban squatters in Delhi*

Though the authorities have programmed in the past to meet the urban-squatter and slum problem of the city, the *bustees* have continued to mushroom; rural-to-urban migration is a visibly continuing and expanding process and cannot be stemmed at its source as yet. No sooner has one *bustee* been cleared than others spring up elsewhere.

The extent of the problem involving the squatters is reflected in the housing deficiency (i.e. families without a shelter of their own), measured at 66,088 in 1951, increasing to 103,920 in 1956, and to 140,000 in 1961. The total number of dwellings in the city which are rapidly reaching a state of dilapidation and will soon be declared unfit for habitation (i.e., will have outlived their utility and will need to be replaced) was estimated at 52 per cent of the total in 1961. The percentage of houses registered as being in first-class condition was 6 per cent, and those in reasonable condition, 42 per cent. The Rent Control Act (which limits the rent any owner can receive from his tenants), the high proportion of absentee landlords, and the extremely low rental value of such a high proportion of dwellings, have contributed considerably to the fact that many house-owners refrain from improving the dwellings and allow them to fall into dilapidation.

A survey by the Delhi Development Authority carried out in

5. *Ibid.*

1960 revealed that 42 per cent of the households in the old city area were without water connections, as were 56 per cent in the Motia Khan zone and 46 per cent in the Subzimandi zone. Two-fifths of the households in Old Delhi were without private latrines, and the electricity connections were meagre.

Of the 256,000 squatters in Old Delhi, who live in *jhuggis*, tents, and temporary shack structures, 116,500 were found to be living within the walled city. A large number of unauthorized dwellings have been constructed in defiance of the law, under the stress of long-denied shelter, and are now beginning to constitute a serious challenge to the authority of the local government.

A recent survey of urban Delhi, conducted by the Municipal Planning Authority, showed that 156,000 children of school age (i.e. 5–16 years) were not attending schools and were receiving no education; nearly all were from the slum-squatter colonies.

The average income of families living in the congested areas of Old Delhi was recorded as Rs. 162–170 (US$32–34) per month; approximately 40 per cent of households in Old Delhi had monthly incomes of less than Rs. 100 (US$20), and 36 per cent had incomes between Rs. 100 and Rs. 200.

Rental capacity for many is less than Rs. 10 per month (i.e. US$2), and providing suitable accommodation within the amortization capacity of 50 per cent of the families is a very serious problem. Though the amortization rates have been considerably reduced, an endeavour to upgrade the earning capacity of these people is still necessary if they are to meet the requirements of regular rentals.

In recent years, with the over-saturation of population in the congested central area, the rural in-migrants, each group consisting of several hundred families, have established large *bustees* on the periphery of the built-up area of the metropolitan city. Usually, the squatter families settle on unused government land or on the vacant lands of absentee landlords. The huts they build are often of solid stone material, each family building its own wall of demarcation, some larger and more permanent than others. With the excessively hot summers and the cold winters, the families sleep out of doors in summer and indoors in winter.

Delhi
Above—A typical *bustee.*
Below—Typical "commercial squatter" groups established on the main
approach roads from the west.

Added to the large *bustee* colonies are the "commercial squatter" groups, who (in combination exerting sufficient influence to gain political support) have set up their craft industries on vacant land adjacent to the approach highways of the city. Some of the groups have the appearance of being nomadic, living in caravan-homes, with their bullocks and tools of trade (for instance, metal-working apparatus, with small forges, or wood-working equipment) always with them, but never paying rent or taxes to the authority. Other groups of commercial squatters have survived for long enough to have set up machinery for undertaking joinery, door- and window-making, etc.

(c) *The squatter resettlement programme*

Slum-squatter clearance in itself, without a continuing follow-up support programme for training and assisting the displaced families towards an improved way of life, is regarded by the authorities of Delhi as being negative in its approach, since it only shifts the problem to another location and another time.

Within a planning framework for the entire country, an urbanization programme for Delhi has been compiled by the Delhi Development Authority (a national government agency) and the Municipal Corporation.

The Delhi authorities have classified the land areas of the city for "conservation", "rehabilitation", and "redevelopment", according to their degree of deterioration and obsolescence, and the families, whether slum-dwellers or squatters, are being absorbed into the urbanization programme.

The present urban squatter population within the confines of the old city is being dealt with within a concept of urban redevelopment, which means that an area or zone of the city becomes by statutory declaration an "area for redevelopment"; such an area is defined as being characterized by "acute congestion, dilapidated housing, intermingling of incompatible land uses, resulting in unwholesome living conditions and gross inadequacy of basic civic amenities and communal facilities".[6] These areas are both economically and physically beyond

6. *Ibid.*

repair, unlike the "rehabilitation areas", which are the partially blighted localities where slum conditions prevail, but which can be converted into healthy neighbourhoods by some judicious planning, such as the realignment of streets, and the clearing of areas for parks, open spaces, etc.

Of the total area of 4,481 acres, with a population of 1,001,403, in the old city, 3,174 acres (accommodating 754,594 persons) were scheduled for either redevelopment or rehabilitation, because of their deteriorated condition.

The degree of obsolescence of any district was based on the following criteria, and weighted in assessment as indicated:

	Factor of Weighting
(a) the number of families resident in the zone with an income of less than Rs.100 per month (US$13)	1
(b) the percentage of poor structures	2
(c) the percentage of households without water	1
(d) the percentage of households without latrines	1
(e) the percentage of households without electricity	0.75
(f) the percentage of households without kitchens	0.75
(g) average number of persons per living room	1

Each item was weighted arithmetically to its considered importance; the condition of structure was considered most important, whilst electricity was weighted as least important. If any zone or area had more than 75 per cent with poor structures, it was marked for redevelopment.

Inside the walled city, 535.6 acres (accommodating 196,865 persons) were scheduled for redevelopment because their existing conditions were those of extreme congestion and filth, constituting a menace to the health of the entire city. The average gross density in these areas was 363 persons per acre, rising to over 500 persons per acre in some sections.

The authorities in 1966 adopted a programme of relocation of some squatter families as part of the urban renewal programme, all of which was an integral part of the general redevelopment plan for the city and the region, rather than a programme of slum clearance only.

Mobility in relation to work has been considered a significant factor in the relocation of the slum squatters, for they must be near the places where they can hope to obtain some means of employment. Surveys show that 46 per cent of the wage-earners in the old city have places of employment well within one mile of travel from their living area.

Where major clearance of high-density slum-squatter colonies is involved, relocation schemes are invoked, and "transit camps" and "urban villages" are established for the temporary accommodation of the families until they are permanently settled in one of the several public housing projects now under construction.

Delhi
    A transit camp for displaced squatters, located, as such camps usually are, close to a new housing-industrial estate. Note ablutions block and wash rooms on the right, and the permanent appearance of some of the cottages.

The construction plans of the Municipal Authority are for multi-story apartments, planned in groups which form a neighbourhood adjacent to easily accessible manufacturing and commercial work centres, including "flatted" industrial centres or estates. The principle is that, as far as possible, such an arrangement will help to maintain opportunities for the people to sustain their earning capacity. Many industries from the congested slum areas are being encouraged to re-establish themselves in the new industrial estates. The transition camps nearby provide temporary accommodation for their former workers until the housing projects are completed.

The financing of these projects, phase by phase, lot by lot, provides a basis for a controlled economic investment programme within the normal financial budgeting procedure of the master development plan and that of the Municipal Corporation. Within such a phased development programme, the extent of national government support, whether by loan or subsidy, is made clear.

The urban villages located on the outskirts or fringes are intended to act as receiving centres for industrial enterprises, and provide both normal industrial activities and those related directly to rural craft or activity. There are many industrial processes in the over-congested areas which are already frustrated in their economic expansion, but which, if moved with their workers from the same congested area to an urban village, could continue the normal process of expansion and growth with little interruption. There would be some economic loss to the industry during the transition stage, and a method for providing compensation payment, or assistance of some kind, was under study in 1966.

New housing schemes are an integral part and prerequisite of the relocation schemes; apart from the multi-story apartment dwellings, provision is also made for some civic amenities, community and social facilities for the people, as part of the project. The sites selected for urban villages are usually located on the fringe of the existing spread of settlement, where water, sewerage, electricity, and other public services can be extended to them at nominal charge.

In all the relocation programmes, the transit camps are considered to be the first step in the programme. The transit camp is intended to be a place of temporary accommodation of reasonable standards; the penalty for not providing such a camp or station during a slum-squatter clearance programme is the dislocation of family cohesion and community life, and much social frustration to the families, the fruits of which are invariably resistance and reaction to future programmes.

In slum clearance programmes, these camps are established as near as possible to the cleared areas, so that the inhabitants

Delhi
   New low-cost housing projects to accommodate urban squatters,
   situated on the periphery of the built-up area, in close proximity to an
   industrial estate and existing transit camps.

can continue their old family associations. The camps are equipped with public services, such as ablution facilities for hygiene, incinerators, paved streets with proper drainage, refuse collection, etc. There is usually a Social Hall, where special training courses are conducted by the authorities for the former slum-dwellers as the first step towards teaching them co-operative and healthy urban living.

The camps are under the guidance of trained community organization workers, who specialize in selecting and promoting local leadership. Where possible, assistance is given in finding employment for the occupants, but much of the effort is aimed at orientating the families towards living in their new houses or apartments, at making them aware of their moral obligations to each other and to the others in the building block as a whole, and of their rent-paying obligations, and, generally, at preparing the families for living in the new housing projects.

The Municipal Corporation of Delhi is setting aside thirteen sites, ranging in area from 20 acres to 200 acres, for the establishment of "reception villages" or "temporary accommodation sites" for those squatters who continue to migrate in from the rural areas. These villages will be prepared with wash-rooms, latrines, water supply, and community and training rooms where the community organizer can provide the occupants with advice, training, and orientation classes for urban living, and, in the case of some of the larger projects, some training in a craft or skill to upgrade the earning capacity of the inhabitants, and assist in their assimilation into the life of the city.

Facilities will be provided for teaching the womenfolk trades and crafts, and an endeavour made to channel idle manpower into productive work, to eradicate illiteracy, and inculcate in the former slum-dweller new attitudes towards urban living.

The programme calls for the co-ordination of governmental and non-governmental resources, and working arrangements are being explored towards this end. Encouraging citizen participation in the redevelopment process is regarded as essential for the ultimate success of the programme. There are no strict criteria or rules laid out for mobilizing citizen participation except perhaps that of fostering civic leadership, an attitude of mind where people are motivated only by objective good will for the well-being of the community, and contribute voluntarily to the common good.

The Municipal Corporation of Delhi has encouraged the formation of a citizen committee in each of the redevelopment areas, which will constitute a link between the planning officials and those who are being planned for. The committees are formed at the various levels of the community groups, with their leaders on the neighbourhood committees. On the committees, every endeavour is made to have representatives from the various interested groups — property-owners, traders, industrialists, co-operative societies, unions, etc., along with experienced leaders in the social, civic, and religious spheres. The people's views are presented by the former, and specific functions are executed by the latter.

The Delhi Municipal Corporation plans to establish the committees as *Vikas Mandals*,[7] which will have jurisdiction over approximately 250 families. Ten *Vikas Mandals* are grouped together to form a neighbourhood council, which, together

---

7. For a comprehensive case study of the formation, organization, progress, and achievement of the *Vikas Mandals* in Delhi, see Marshall B. Clinard, *Slums and Community Development: Experiments in Self-Help* (New York: Free Press, 1966).

with the welfare agencies and civic administration, forms the advisory committee.

The foundations have been laid for gradually upgrading manpower and for the continuing assimilation of the urban squatter into established urban society.

HOUSING POLICY TO ACCOMMODATE URBAN SQUATTERS

One example of a country approaching the urban squatter problem on the basis of a long-range national housing programme is that of Turkey.

The 1964 survey carried out by the Social Research Department of the Ministry of Reconstruction and Resettlement in Turkey determined that in Ankara, the national capital and a city of nearly one million persons, 70,000 dwellings (accommodating more than 400,000 persons) were occupied by squatters.[8]

8. *Urbanization and Housing Situation in Turkey* (Ministry of Reconstruction and Settlement, Social Research Study No. 2 [Ankara, 1966]), p. 54.

Turkey
  A typical *gecekondu* and squatter family on the outskirts of Istanbul.
  (Photograph taken 1967.)

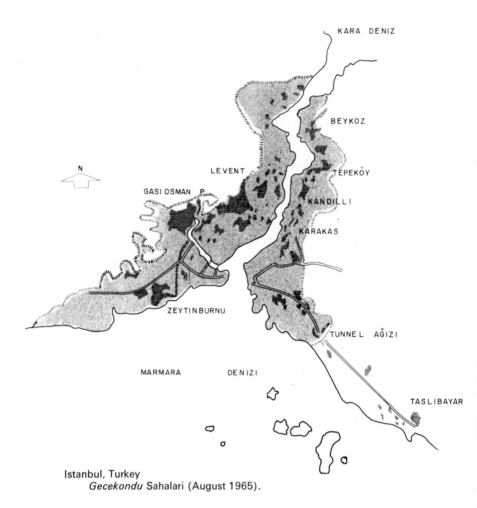

Istanbul, Turkey
  Gecekondu Sahalari (August 1965).

The government acknowledges that "the squatter houses
are already attached to the city, and the inhabitants form part
of the city population ... from their density and standards,
they have all the characteristics of slums".[9] Though they have
been built in violation of the building laws and regulations,
they constitute such a high proportion of the population of
each city in the country that the government, with its declared
policy of providing a home for every family (commencing

9. *Ibid.*

with the lowest income group), proposes to improve those *gecekondus* which can be improved, some with grants and some on a public loan basis, and ultimately to provide the occupants with the title to the land; for those areas which are beyond rehabilitation, the government intends to reaccommodate the squatter families in social housing schemes.

Another project, and one of the best demonstrations of squatter clearance through an effective low-cost high-density housing programme, can be viewed in Hong Kong.

The Government of Hong Kong had to deal with the problem of waves of migrants entering the colony from mainland China. Over the seven-year period 1949–1956, the authorities estimate that the number of squatters increased ten times, or from approximately 30,000 to approximately 300,000; their numbers were continuing to increase annually thereafter at the same rate.[10]

The squatter colonies in Hong Kong, as in most other cities, sprang in the first place from a small nucleus, and grew to their own colony saturation level, which appears to range between 50,000 and 100,000; it was estimated that 80,000 were accommodated in the Shek Kip Mei squatter colony in 1953. Many of the squatter shacks grew and continued to multiply around the periphery of Kowloon, i.e. on the mainland side, and by 1953 had formed an almost solid "squatter fence" around the city, prejudicing the normal economic and physical expansion of the city. The squatter colonies had already established their own factories, opium dens, and market centres, along with their own leadership and security hierarchy. The regular city police could exercise little effective jurisdiction within these areas. During Christmas 1953 the fireworks factory in Shek Kip Mei exploded, and fire swept through the whole squatter colony; 50,000 persons were rendered homeless overnight.

A Department of Resettlement was immediately created by the government, and the Department of Public Works was entrusted with the design and immediate construction of six-story walk-up apartments; each family was allocated a room of 120 square feet, the allocation being based on the standard of 24 square feet per adult person (children under ten years of age were allocated 12 square feet). Each floor was

10. *Hong Kong Annual Report* (1956), p. 16.

Hong Kong
Typical urban squatter colony. (Photograph taken 1962.)

provided with communal washrooms, laundry space, cooking space, and toilets. Considering that the average standard of accommodation in their former squatter colony was measured at 8 square feet per adult person, without convenient water supply or provision for sanitation, the resettlement project went a long way towards raising their standard of living. The resettlement apartments were constructed at the same density as the squatter colonies had covered the land, i.e. 2,000 persons per acre. Rising to six floors, there was plenty of space on the ground floor for the families to continue their crafts and trades, and before long the access balconies, by mutual under-standing, were also used for home industry. With the simple repetitive design, the Public Works Department was able to complete each 420-room resettlement building in eight weeks.

The resettlement buildings were intended only for those families of very low income who could afford little for rent. With the relocation of the families displaced by the fire, the authorities recognized that many of the squatter families were industrious and could afford to pay rent for a larger and better apartment, if such were available.

In 1954, the Hong Kong Housing Authority was inaugurated, with an initial loan from the Government of Hong Kong of $156 million (HK$7.1 = US$1), which has since been converted into a revolving fund. The land for the housing projects was provided by the government and subsidized to half its commercial value, and the loans were made available at forty years' amortization at $3\frac{1}{2}$ per cent interest. This meant that rentals for an apartment of 350 square feet could be reduced to HK$14 per month (i.e. less than US$3 per month).

In co-operation with the Resettlement Department and the Public Works Department, the Authority had accommodated a total of 600,000 former urban squatters in housing units, mostly apartments, by 1965 (i.e. over the eleven-year period). The Authority adopted density standards of 1,600 to 2,000 persons per acre, and immediately established an effective organization to be responsible for housing management and tenant education.

Each project was provided with high schools, primary schools, communal rooms and halls, shopping and commercial centres, post offices, and play areas. Each apartment was

Hong Kong
    Typical Housing Authority projects, density of accommodation being
approximately 2,000 persons per acre. (Photograph taken 1962.)

Hong Kong
Squatter resettlement buildings, showing space between buildings for communal use. (Photograph taken 1962.)

self-contained, and the standard of accommodation was raised to 35 square feet per person. Play space for the children was provided on each floor. Management took responsibility for the maintenance of property, refuse collection, cleanliness of grounds, car parks, rent collection, and renting out and organizing the use of communal spaces. It also assisted in the solving of domestic problems.[11]

The housing estates were designed in such a way that they comprised integrated neighbourhood units, all of which formed part of a larger built-up community or district, and provided an opportunity for the occupants to enjoy the day-to-day environment of a normal daily life.

[11] Hong Kong Housing Authority, *Annual Report* (1961–1962).

Priority of occupancy was given to families living in the resettlement projects who had made application for improved accommodation, and whose members were obviously industrious. The Authority found that, with selected tenancy and the low rentals, not only was there little or no delinquency in the payment of rents, but the occupants assisted in the maintenance of the building; they were able to accumulate savings and establish their way of life more satisfactorily; their morale was usually high, and many preferred and applied for larger apartments. In the first ten years of its operation, the Housing Authority had accommodated 130,000 in these apartments, estates such as So Uk and Choi Hung accommodating nearly 13,000 persons each.

Hong Kong
The squatters integrated into the urban scene. The resettlement buildings have taken the place of the squatter colony. (Photograph taken 1962.)

LAND AND UTILITY PROJECTS FOR URBAN SQUATTERS

One government which made a start towards officially acknowledging the pressure of human need on the urban land surrounding the city and endeavoured to legalize the occupation of this land by the squatters is the Government of Peru. This did not happen, however, until the rising tide of squatter invasion onto private and government land became too much for the police forces, which tried to repel the "land invasions" in a determined and often violent way.

The story of the squatter settlements of Peru has been clearly told by Dr. William Mangin, Syracuse University,[12] who has lived with the *barriadas* and made a comprehensive study of the people and their problem. He described how the *barriadas* of Lima had their beginning in the years immediately following World War II; how it was usual for the police to drive the families from the land by force, "sometimes with fatal beatings of the men, women and children, and then burning their shacks and household goods". This only caused the *barriadas* to organize themselves on a quasi-military basis. Only married couples under thirty years of age were recruited, and their leaders were highly intelligent and articulate.

Members of their organization, who knew something of the system of land registration, searched the government land titles offices for sites of land owned by a public agency, preferably the national government. The organizers then visited the site at night and demarcated the lots, usually with the help of university architectural and engineering students, assigning some lots to members of the association for homes, other lots for schools, churches, shops, streets, etc., and working always in the utmost secrecy to avoid police interference. When all had been agreed upon amongst themselves, and the day of the "invasion" drew near, the organizers confidentially approached leading political personalities and religious leaders to solicit support for their invasion, and they also ensured maximum newspaper coverage to witness and publish any signs and evidence of police brutality.

12. William Mangin, "Squatter Settlements", *Scientific American,* October 1967, pp. 21–29.

Usually several hundred families were involved in each such invasion, and each time the action was apparently so spontaneous and so well organized, and the families so numerous, that it was beyond the capacity of the police either to impede or evict the families, once in occupation; more than a hundred such invasions to set up *barriadas* have taken place in Peru in the past twenty years. The squatters around the cities of Peru numbered 700,000 in 1967, 450,000 of them living in the *barriadas* of Lima itself.

Dr. Mangin discovered, after his personal investigation of the *barriadas*, that, contrary to the generally held belief of the authorities (which was that the squatters were uneducated, unambitious, disorganized, and an economic drag on the nation), they were generally "organized, politically sophisticated, strongly patriotic and comparatively conservative in their socio-political views. Although poor, they do not live the life of squalor and hopelessness characteristic of the culture of poverty, depicted by Oscar Lewis". The families improve their shacks and begin to build in solid materials as soon as they can accumulate some money from any form of employment they can obtain.

Many have consolidated their community structure to include painted houses with elegant fronts, stores, banks, and movie-houses; yet despite this (and the appearance of refrigerators and television sets), the earning capacity of the *barriada* families collectively is still insufficient to finance the installation of a piped water supply or drainage-sewerage system; "water and fuel (mainly kerosene) are transported in bottles or drums by truck, bicycle or on foot." Some individual generators provide electricity to small groups of families.

What is significant in the social composition of the *barriadas* is that often a small group of professional people (attorneys, bank managers, etc. — a creative minority) are found to be members of the associations or clubs.

The associations of the *barriadas*, in common with similar associations in Venezuela and Brazil, levy a tax on the members, organize co-operative projects, act as arbitrators for internal disputes, endeavour to negotiate collectively with the local authority, and organize local security for their members.

The majority of the occupants commute to the city of Lima

for employment, working in personal services, factories, stores, etc.

Schooling for the children is mostly available only in the city of Lima, but there is an occasional example where the residents of a *barriada* have organized their own elementary school.

Following a practice common to all squatter colonies throughout the world, some of the original "invaders" have rented out, traded, or sold the "right" to their lot, drawing up their own deeds of negotiation within the purview of their own association, although such documents are not recognized by the law of the land.

The *barriada* families enjoy a better community stability than is usually found in the city slums or rural villages: "prostitution and delinquency, common in the city slums, were rare in the barriadas."[13]

The organized squatter associations made a plea to the government for recognition of their plight, and the need for decent homes of their own; the President of Peru appointed a special commission in 1956 to investigate and draw up a programme for implementation.

The commission recognized the value of the human resources and initiative of the *barriadas*, along with the "real value" of the houses which they had already built, many of them being constructed of stone and solid material. The commission drafted a law which authorized the government to acquire the land from the owners compulsorily, at fair market price, and to arrange for the transfer to the squatters of the title to the land on which they were situated, after they had paid in full both the value of the land and the value of public services and improvements such as water supply, electricity, drainage and sewerage,[14] when these were provided.

A law was adopted by the Peruvian State Legislature in 1957 which authorized the granting of the land titles to *barriada* dwellers. It took some time for this to take effect, and when some titles were finally issued for some of the *barriada* associa-

13. *Ibid.*
14. John C. Turner, *Uncontrolled Urban Settlements: Problems and Policies* (Report for the United Nations Seminar on Urbanization [Pittsburg, 1966]).

tions, the titles were marked "provisional".[15] The precedent was set, however, for the rehabilitation of urban squatters *in situ*, with legislative support, whether on State or private land.

The principle of organized take-over of private lands by organized urban squatter groups has spread around the world. In 1964, 1,000 families, during a long week-end, moved into a 30–hectare tract of private land on the fringes of the city of Manila, in the Philippines. In less than a week, the families were well installed, with light and water connections. The owner of the land failed to obtain an eviction order from the Court, and the colony has since prospered.

COMMUNITY DEVELOPMENT TECHNIQUES APPLIED TO SQUATTER REHABILITATION

Experiments in techniques for rehabilitating urban squatters *in situ* were taken a step further by the Centro Interamericano de Vivienda y Planeamiento (CINVA), Bogota, Colombia, in 1956, under the directorship of Mr. Eric Carlson.

As exercises for the postgraduate scholars, several projects and programmes were conducted under controlled conditions of experiment and observation. One case study, the squatter colony in Siloe, Cali, a city of Colombia, is an interesting indication of the response patterns which can be expected from the urban squatter families to a project designed for the improvement of their environment.

CINVA, though not able to become involved in the transfer of land titles as demonstrated in the "land and utilities" projects of Lima, did endeavour to develop the human resources factor of the community and so introduced a new technique into the treatment of the urban squatter problem. This was El Proceso de Desarrollo Comunal Aplicado a um Proyecto de Rehabilitacion Urbana, or the process of community development applied to an urban renewal project, the full report of which is available from CINVA, Bogota.

The motivation for this concept originated from the Department of Preventive Medicine and Public Health of the Medical

15. Mangin, *op. cit.*

Faculty of the University of Valle, Colombia, and the project soon won the support of the regional and local authorities and the participation of CINVA. The municipal authorities of Siloe, a district in the city of Cali, in Colombia, were concerned about the large proportion of urban squatters in their city population, and collaborated in the experiment, as did many non-governmental agencies and church groups, who were equally concerned in the welfare of their fellow citizens.

A careful socio-economic survey of family circumstances of the selected squatter colony was undertaken, and an indication was obtained of the willing response and likely participation of the squatter families in a programme designed to improve the circumstances of their environmental sanitation.

The site of the squatter colony occupied 43 hectares, with an average slope of 30°, and was (as is so often the case in the Latin American cities which were former Spanish colonies) *ejido*, meaning that it was land which a large landholder had conceded to the city for common use by poor families, the ownership of the land always remaining with the former title-holder. The number of persons in the colony was estimated to be approximately 25,000, i.e. a density of nearly 600 persons per hectare.

Approximately 50 per cent of the adults were literate, but had received no secondary education. Nevertheless, many heads of households were skilled in some trade or craft, and received a reasonable level of income, though comparatively low. On the whole, the families had already begun the urban assimilation process on their own, and all that was required was a rationalization of their status, upgrading of their living standards and community environmental sanitation circumstances, and ultimately acquisition of title of ownership to the land on which they were situated.

The various families had migrated into this squatter colony over a period of many years; the exploitation of some of the local coal mines, in combination with easy access to this site for resettlement purposes, is suggested as the origin of the squatter colony. Water for the community was being hand-carried daily by the menfolk from local springs; the nearby river provided both the site and the water for their laundry.

At the commencement of the project, family cohesion, and provincial and group loyalties (within the *compadrazzo* system) were well established, and there existed a clearly defined leadership pattern for carrying out the exercise.

As is typical in so many cases of urban squatter colonies throughout Latin America, the families were already formed into their own self-help groups. Many families had some form of employment, and on an average their family income was about the equivalent of US$30 a month; many had a savings capacity, which was set aside for home and communal improvement projects. They paid no land taxes or rent to the city, and therefore received no public services.

They had, as a group of people, already evolved in their desire for self-improvement and community progress to the point that leadership and guidance in method was all that was required. They exercised their own security and police arrangements, which is standard practice in almost all squatter colonies. Many of the houses had been erected overnight in a crude form, but, as interference from the local authority proved to be no hazard, some in course of time had added to their dwellings and constructed them of more solid material. In the end, entry of a family into the colony was only through negotiation, and always through the *compadrazzo* system, around which the local security was organized.

At the time CINVA began the exercise, i.e. in 1956, many of the houses were still only one-roomed shacks, 60 square feet in area, accommodating an entire family of five or six persons; some were constructed of bamboo, paper, and mud whilst others, in contrast, were built in adobe and brick. Wood and kerosene were used as fuel for cooking and lighting.

As with the "community development" approach, the research teams identified the problems of the colony as they were expressed by:

(a) the inhabitants of the colony;
(b) the municipal authorities; and
(c) as recognized and defined from the results of the survey and synthesis of the information of (a) and (b) above.

The replies given by the inhabitants of the community, expressed through their committees and those recognized by the local authorities, are observed to be almost the same as those pertaining to the majority of squatter colonies around the world, involving millions of families on the fringes of, and sometimes within, the built-up area of many of the great cities.

The synthesis of the information on Cali revealed:

(a) *Problems Felt by the Community*
   Lack of drinking water
   Lack of drainage
   Uncollected rubbish
   Deficient roads
   Lots held illegally, instead of by right of title
   Insufficient medical care
   Floods causing landslides and danger to houses and lives
   Insufficient community cohesion amongst neighbours
   Lack of police protection

(b) *Problems Recognized by Authorities*
   Inadequate medical services
   Lack of drinking water
   Malnutrition
   Poor housing
   Deficient roads
   Lack of sewers
   Absence of community services
   Impossibility of collecting land taxes
   Lots illegally held
   Neighbourhood communities not represented
   Neighbourhood land values adversely affected

The survey team from CINVA, after intensive field studies of the circumstances, confirmed and synthesized the problems expressed above.

A programme of community improvement was then drawn up, and the process of organizing the self-help work-groups around this programme began. Natural leadership patterns began to emerge, often different from those already established under the *compadrazzo* system, and formal negotiations were commenced with the local authority for proper representation from the squatter colony with the council. In the second year of

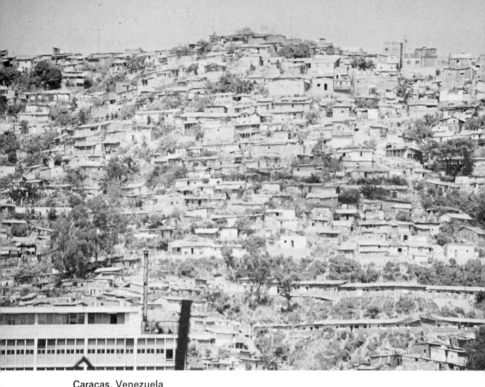

Caracas, Venezuela
Above—Typical urban squatter colonies. (Photograph taken 1967.)
Below—Housing projects to combat the urban squatter problem.

operation, much communal and home improvement had already been achieved. Public services were being provided by the local authorities, for which arrangements for payment had been completed, and mutual agreement and respect prevailed between the occupants of the squatter colony (as an organized and recognized group of families) and the local authority.

The municipality had then before it the task of negotiating the transfer of land titles from the present owners to the residents of the squatter colony. These negotiations are still going on.

Similar stories can be told of the squatter problem in other countries throughout Latin America, such as Venezuela, and Chile, particularly regarding the use of community development techniques as the vehicle for upgrading, consolidating, and assimilating the urban squatter into organized and established urban society.

RECUPERATION OF URBAN SQUATTER COLONIES

The favelas in Rio de Janeiro – Background

One of the inheritances of all Latin American countries on gaining independence was the Spanish or Portuguese land tenure and title system. With its liberal disposal of land under the "Friar lands" system, and land granted as a court favour, the registration of the land was by no means always clear or accurate, either as to the titleholder or in its cadastral plotting, with the result that the judiciary in many countries is having to decide between claimants possessing old Spanish titles covering land registered to cover approximately the same area of land, but with the boundaries rarely coinciding. In our present decade, when many of the cities have spread out to meet what was once peripheral grazing and agricultural land, these old titles have taken on an entirely new meaning, monetarily, for urban land values are now so inflated that these titles are literally worth millions of dollars. In many of the cities, and Rio de Janeiro is a case in point, the task of determining the rightful owner of the land on which some of the *favelados* or squatters are living is so complicated and indefinite that the authorities cannot instigate legal proceedings to acquire the land for the purpose of rehabilitating the resident families. In other cases, some land claimants simply bring their own armed wrecking team into the *favela*, order the families out, demolish their shacks, and take over the use of the land, whilst the ownership of the title is still being decided in the courts.[16]

Unlike the squatter colonies of Hong Kong, Manila, and Delhi, which had their beginnings in the immediate post-war era (each for a different reason, but all a consequence of a social upheaval and/or change of governmental status), the *favelas* of Rio de Janeiro had their beginnings in 1910. The new republic had been formed in 1891, but the problems of rural land tenure caused a conflict between the rural communities and the owners of large landholdings. This ultimately caused an uprising, led by Canudos,[17] which, though not successful as an uprising, simply forced a large number of families displaced from the land to migrate in an organized group to Rio de Janeiro and establish the first *favela*.[18]

16.   Observations made by Peace Corps volunteer, M. P. Silberstein, who was a resident in the *favela* at the time.
17.   Euclides da Cunha, *Rebellion in the Backlands*, 1910.
18.   The name *favela* is a botanical term for the root of a flower.

Rio de Janeiro
The first *favela*, originating in 1910.

As the former slaves gained their freedom from the time of the republic, they also had to turn somewhere for a home. Many more *favelas* appeared — at first discreetly in isolated areas on the periphery of the city of Rio. There followed, in the middle 1930's, an even larger influx from the rural areas, as a result of "the coffee crisis" — all searching for employment or some means of livelihood.

During the war years (as in Delhi and many other great cities around the world), rural-to-urban migration began towards all the large cities of Brazil, including those in northern Brazil, where large military, naval, and air force bases were established. Such stations usually provided ample opportunities for remunerative employment. As the city has spread out over the past fifty years, the early *favelas*, which were once on the periphery of the city, have become an integral part of the townscape.

Since the 1939–1945 war, not only have the number of *favelados* consolidated into very densely settled areas, but their actual number has varied from year to year according to the number of *favelas* which have been cleared from any one site, the occupants having been consequently dispersed to establish themselves in new *favelas* on new sites in other parts of the city.

There is no accurate official estimate of the exact total of *favelas* or *favelados* in existence, though the Department of Recuperation of *Favela* Areas, State of Guanabara, released the information to the press in February 1967 that there were 760,000 persons residing in 162,000 makeshift homes in 306 "hillside *favelas*" in Rio de Janeiro at that time.[19] Previously, in 1948, the Instituto Brasileiro de Geografia a Estatística had estimated that there were 103,176 persons in 21,227 *favela* units in Rio de Janeiro. A study of the 1960 census indicates 337,414 persons in *favelas*. A town-planning group estimated their number to be 417,100 at the end of 1964, arriving at this figure from aerial photographs and assuming an average household size of 4.8 persons per visible roof area.

[19.] A survey carried out under the auspices of a commission created by the Federal Government in May 1968 (Coordenação e Habitação de Interêsse Social da Área Metropolitana, within the Ministry of Interior) estimated that there were nearly one million *favelados* throughout the city at that time.

Rio de Janeiro
   Typical hillside *favela*. Approximately three hundred such *favelas* exist,
   accounting for about 20 per cent of the population of the city.
   (Photograph taken 1967.)

However, with some subsequent surveys, it was discovered that many of the roofs housed up to four or more *favela* families, grouped under the common roof in what is known as "gemini" cluster. The estimate therefore can clearly be increased, but to what extent, without a house-to-house survey of each *favela*, is unknown. Another agency, working with the volunteer groups in the *favelas*, estimated the number to be 830,000 persons at that time. In 1961, the Federal Planning and Housing Service agency estimated their number in Rio to be 965,400 persons.

A study group of the Institute of Architects in Brazil reported that, during the floods in Rio de Janeiro in 1966 (and a similar tragedy caught the city unawares in February 1967), 2,400 *favela* dwellings were destroyed, 1,800 damaged, and 3,400 were in imminent danger of collapse; the flash floods left 260 dead and 46,000 homeless. The architects reported that 63 per cent of the shanty towns were almost demolished by landslides and washouts, and were uninhabitable without reassembly.

A recent sample survey carried out in five elementary schools of the six-to-seven-year-old children who lived in the *favelas* revealed that 88 per cent were suffering from malnutrition, 80 per cent from anaemia, 78 per cent from oral infections, and 77 per cent from worms.[20]

The city of Rio de Janeiro is unique in that it has a high urban fence, towering up some 2,000 feet, less than one mile from the shoreline of both the ocean and the harbour. Densities of population vary from 3,500 persons per hectare in Copacabana to 13 persons per hectare in Barra da Tijuca.

On the whole, the density of population in the *favelas* is estimated to vary between 500 and 1,000 persons per hectare. The average density in the built-up area of the city within the State of Guanabara was estimated to be 1,130 persons per square kilometre in 1965, and it is continuing to increase with the growing population.[21]

In recent years the Government of Guanabara has pursued a programme to clear the *favelas*, and in 1962 it began the

20. Hempstone Smith, "Population Drift to Cities Causes Brazilian Slums", *Evening Star* (Washington, D.C.), 24 November 1966.
21. Estimates by the Brazilian Institute of Architects.

clearance and relocation of several selected *favelas*. Several
areas were set aside for the various types of families; one,
Nova Holanda, was intended for the very poor who could afford
little or no rent. It was located on the shores of the harbour,
within easy reach of all places of work in the city. Its purpose
was really that of a transient station for those whose income
was too low to meet the amortization of a low-cost house and
land; little was provided by the authorities, except an allocation
of space per family. A second-stage resettlement area was
established at Vila Esperanca for those with a little more
earning capacity, and who had some opportunity to work in
the city.

The third stage was a new community built at Vila Kennedy,
some 30 kilometres from the centre of Rio, for those who could
afford to amortize a low-income home. A new steel mill was
planned for construction in the vicinity (some 20 kilometres

Brazil
Left—Rio de Janeiro. Typical hillside *favela*.
Below—Vila Kennedy. Squatter relocation project.

away) and was intended to be the source of employment and wealth for the inhabitants of Vila Kennedy. The community (for 2,000 families) was laid out and built with good low-income homes, schools, play areas, and shopping areas, and with streets for the most part paved and kerbed. Tragically, in a nationwide economic slump, the plans to construct the steel mill were discontinued after the families had moved to their new location. An active programme of home and craft industries was undertaken by government and non-government agencies, and this helped the families until the employment crisis eased, and the families were able to readjust themselves in other places of employment in the industrial zone of Rio de Janeiro. Many spend more than two hours daily, travelling to work in Rio.

Through this experience much was learnt, and this has led the authorities to explore the possibility of rehabilitating as many *favelas* as possible on the sites on which they are located.

Non-government agencies and favela rehabilitation techniques

Studies are being carried out at present in Rio de Janeiro regarding the possibility of using this approach in an effort to assimilate some of the *favelados* of Rio into the urban structure of the city.

Some years ago, the government began an experiment aimed at rehabilitating the *favela* Jacarèzinho, which, because the city has physically spread out beyond it, is now contained within the urban spread and built-up area of the city.[22]

Nearly thirty years ago, during the "coffee crisis", families migrated to this site, which was, and still is, State Government land. As the city has spread outwards, industries and places of employment have established themselves close by, until now they almost totally surround the *favela*. Over the years, the site has been filled to the limits of its boundaries with shacks, which, since they have a reasonable income and no rent or taxes to pay, the *favelados* have in turn improved and added to until buildings of stone and concrete have now taken their

22. Observations on Jacarèzinho made in the company of Mr J. Wyggand, Peace Corps volunteer, who was for some time resident in the *favela*.

Rio de Janeiro
Close-up of part of *favela* Jacarèzinho, established in 1930 and now
consolidated into permanent residences. (Photograph taken 1967.)

place. Invariably, families who arrived later and occupied
the lower fringes of the *favela* were, in time, able to negotiate
for the occupancy of one of the more substantially built *favelas*
higher up the slope from a sale of the rights of their former
shack, and a loan from the local *pistolão*. There has been a social
gradation and continuing movement upwards, both literally
and figuratively, by many families from the time of their
arrival. As they have obtained work, and their children have
gone to school, over the decades they have negotiated their
way from the very low-income lower-level zone (physically)
of the site up through the social and income strata to the higher
sections of the hill, which command a view and benefit from
the sea breezes; the houses they occupy are always a highly
negotiable commodity which they invariably improve whilst
they are in occupancy.

Many of the houses are already two-storied and constructed
of reinforced concrete, with concrete block walls, and with a
flat concrete roof ready for the addition of another floor.

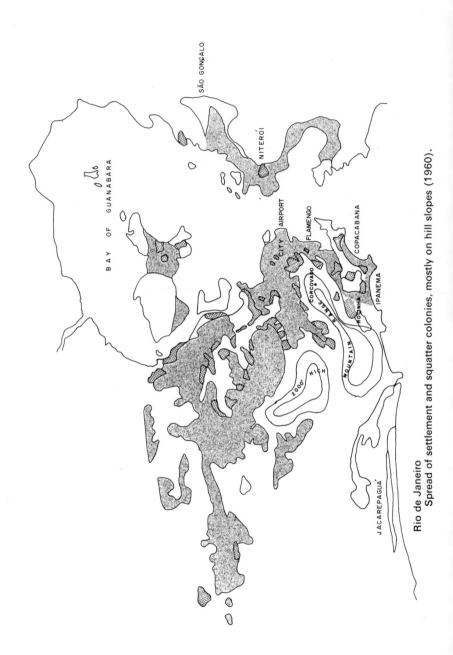

Rio de Janeiro
Spread of settlement and squatter colonies, mostly on hill slopes (1960).

A water-main passes contiguously with the site on the higher level, and with a little overnight engineering a tapping was made, which, despite continual attempts by the authorities to sever the connection, continues to provide the entire *favela* of 50,000 persons with an adequate water supply free of cost, except for their own costs of installation. Electricity was connected by the *pistolão*, who negotiated a bulk supply, and now distributes and sells the power (reportedly at a much higher rate than is usual for the city).

Much the same applies to the markets in the *favelas*; the sale of commodities is under the control of only a few persons, who usually procure low-quality vegetables fruits, meats, etc.

These are the signs of the self-urbanization process of this particular *favela*; probably much of the moral advancement can be attributed to the leadership of the priest of the *favela*, who now has many of the families contributing to and helping in the construction of a large reinforced concrete church, in which education for the children is provided in rooms on the lower ground floor.

It is acknowledged that up to ten years ago, before the employment situation was stable, the *favela* was the haunt and hide-out (as is often the case in urban squatter colonies) of criminals and rough gangs, who extracted "tithes" or "tong" from the inhabitants of the *favela*, through intimidation. As is the case in most *favelas* and urban squatter colonies, the security of the area was the responsibility of the occupants. A *favela* association was formed, and, by "group action" of the established families, the notorious characters, or any persons who could not submit to the rules of peaceable coexistence, were forcibly expelled from the *favela*. The association then invited the police force of the district to establish a police station in the *favela*, and from that time on, for approximately the past ten years, the energies of many of the populace have been directed towards the construction of the church, and the pursuit of education and collective self-advancement.

The association requested the State Government to assist them in rehabilitating the *favela*. A main access road was laid out, and a programme for proper water connection, community welfare and development work, medical and dental services, etc. was undertaken. There is sign of much progress towards this end, although with the change in the political party of the State Government after an election in 1964 there was a slowing down of the *favela* rehabilitation projects. But in 1968, the Federal Government intervened, and a special commission, Coordenação Habitacional de Interêsse Social da Área Metropolitana (CHISAM), which had representatives from the Ministry of Interior, National Housing Bank, and the two State Governments of Guanabara and Rio de Janeiro, was created.

Rio de Janeiro
> The approach to *favela* Rocinha. Detail of small section, as it mounts the hill. More than 80,000 persons live in this colony. Because of confusion over the ownership of the title to the land, the State cannot acquire the land for resettlement. There is no water supply, no sewerage, no drainage connections to dwellings.

Rio de Janeiro
Favela rising up the slopes behind the high-density apartment buildings on Copacabana beach.

A revolving fund of the approximate equivalent of US$50 million was established, and the programme of *favela* recuperation, plus an extensive low-cost housing programme, has now been greatly accelerated.

The role of the non-governmental agencies in assisting the social development of a great number of the *favelados* is most noticeable. A case in point is that of the *favela* of Rocinha,[23] a *favela* of some 75,000 persons, which is at present on the periphery of the built-up area of the city and, in fact, is located on the extension of the famous Copacabana and Leblon beaches; already, high-value development is extending beyond this *favela* along the coastline. The houses of the *favela* are situated on the steep slopes of this valley and command a most enviable view of the beaches and the coastline, a view of much scenic value.

[23]. Observations on *favela* Rocinha made in the company of Dr. Oswaldo Bittencourt Sampaio, Co-ordinator, Planning and Budgeting, State of Guanabara, a leader of the group of citizens who had established the training centre for the *favela*.

Manaus, Brazil
  Above—Typical riverside squatter huts.
  Below—Typical riverside squatter huts. The river level rises up to the level of the duckboards for two months every year.

Because of the confusion over the ownership of the title to the land, the authorities can take no action to improve the circumstances of the site, but a group of leading citizens has formed a society and raised funds to provide a vocational training centre for those families who volunteer for training.

A large communal hall, well equipped with facilities for teaching carpentry, sewing, handcrafts, kitchen and home economics, home and personal hygiene, and domestic service, has been built and is operated on a volunteer basis.

Members of the society have arranged for medical services to the *favela* at weekends, and they also provide special classes in building trades for the young men who are not gainfully employed. The society is already assisting the families in the realignment of some of the shacks to improve the drainage and environmental sanitation problem of the area; water is obtained from springs in the valley itself. The State Government has provided an elementary school on adjacent government land, and a bus company runs regular services from the *favela* to a point connecting with most other bus routes throughout the city of Rio.

The *favela* association has established its own employment bureau, and every Monday morning, and sometimes on other mornings, the "jobs available" for which the association has been contacted or which the association has been able to negotiate, are announced to the residents of the *favela* through a loudspeaker system; applicants are checked by the association before they proceed to the city for their work, whether it be in domestic service, the building trades, or some other avenue of employment.

In almost all of the *favelas*, there is one to whom most of the *favelados* turn for advice, loans of money, etc., and he is known as the *pistolão*. Often he is assisted by the *cabo eleitoral*, who arranges support for politicians from the *favelados*. The *favela* association usually arranges for the local security of the *favela* and for marketing rights, and, in order to sustain its operational funds, levies an occasional local tax on the inhabitants.

Up to some years ago the *cabo eleitoral* ranked very highly in the *favelas* of Rio de Janeiro; the *favelados* placed much confidence in the promises of the politicians who visited their *favelas*, inspected their living conditions, and made promises for their improvement. This invariably took place just before the elections, and promises were conditional upon the *favelados* giving the politician their votes. However, little evidence of improvement was noticed by the *favelados*, who conceded that their elected representative was being pressed too much with other matters of state to deal with their problem, a state of affairs which seemed to prevail until just before the next election, when again there would be more promises made. In very recent years, the importance of the *cabo eleitoral* in the *favelas* of Rio has dwindled, with the result that most of the associations have lost confidence in the present system of political representation, and, not expecting much improvement in their circumstances from this source, are becoming more personally determined to improve their plight through their own capacity and united efforts.

Rio de Janeiro
   Note the large "patch" of urban squatters adjacent to the recreation
   centres of this section of the city. The *favela* was known as Praia do
   Pinto —— it was cleared by the Government in 1969.

There are many other cases amongst the *favelas* in Rio de Janeiro where non-governmental societies have been formed specifically to sponsor medical care, child welfare, adult education, and social development. An interesting case in point is the *ambulatório* of the *favela* of Praia do Pinto, a *favela* of 11,000 people. Founded some fifteen years ago by an Episcopalian priest, the society has regular programmes for raising the funds to maintain a full-time medical, child welfare, and social services centre. One of the sources of their funds is a Gala Ball, held each year under the patronage of the British Ambassador and his wife.

Many of the *favelas* retain a "*samba* school" and qualify for a subsidy which is provided annually by the government office responsible for the *Rio Carnaval*. This annual climax of their lives, brightened by their own endeavours to compose the prize-winning *samba* of the carnival, is a stimulus which helps to retain a close social cohesion within the *favelas*.

The *favelas* of Rio have also attracted the attention of the American Peace Corps. Many Peace Corps volunteers have lived in the different *favelas*, helping the community in different ways, and can now be considered as having consolidated a useful compendium of information which can be applied towards the *favela* rehabilitation programme.

There are, in fact, many private non-governmental groups at work among the *favelas*, and, though no assessment has yet been made of the value of their contribution in combined effort, it can be assumed to be very large. Yet another example is that of Ação Comunitária do Brasil, which was organized by a group of industrial and professional men. Apart from regular donations from all over Brazil, they have received pledges of support from thirty United States companies which have offices in Rio de Janeiro. The objectives of Ação are "to create stable self-reliant communities capable of developing their own improvement programmes of self-help in education, physical improvements, recreation and health, all depending upon the needs and priorities set by the people of the *favelas* themselves".[24]

There are, however, energetic rural development projects being developed by the government, which are aimed at

24. News release, *Brazil Herald*, Friday, 17 March 1967, p. 2.

stemming some of the flow of rural migrants to the cities by planning and developing new agrarian communities, all complete with their local urban facilities. It is expected that over the next twenty years these planned agrarian nucleii, based on the settlement-supporting capacity of the land and related to their own various spheres of influence within a planned settlement pattern across the region, will in themselves become the counter-magnets of the cities and absorb some of the rural-to-urban migration flow, thereby retaining a higher factor of population on the land and taking urbanization back into the rural areas.

CHAPTER THREE

A Case Study of Urban Squatter Relocation in the Philippines

THE BEGINNINGS OF SQUATTING IN MANILA

Upon the cessation of hostilities in 1945, and as a result of the widespread devastation of countryside and cities during the liberation (added to the destruction of the rural economy during the war years), thousands of homeless families migrated into Manila in 1945 and began to settle there, erecting temporary shelters on any vacant lots, or utilizing any existing shelters amongst the ruins, with little if any regard to land ownership. So began urban squatting in Manila.

The rehabilitation of the city and the task of restoring it to normal life was in the hands of a newly created civil government; the independence of the Philippines had been negotiated with the United States Government in 1935, and was to have come into effect in 1945. The newly created independent government was faced with the problems of disrupted public services, many official records destroyed, and a disorganized civil service. Initially the army played a major role in assisting the government to re-establish public services, and to restore normal life to the city; it is, therefore, no surprise that thousands of families wandered back into the city to set up their temporary shelters near the army camps which were established in and around the city, since they felt that here there was some hope of obtaining employment and food.

These circumstances, in the early post-war days, brought
about a recognition by the government that urban housing
should be an important function of government. Soon after
civil government was once again established and functioning,
steps were taken to merge the People's Homesite Corporation
with the National Housing Commission, to become the People's
Homesite and Housing Corporation (PHHC), the national
housing instrumentality. [1]

In 1947, the Corporation adopted a procedure for raffling
home lots for the homeless families on a portion of their property
in Quezon City, which is contiguous with the City of Manila.
Upon a petition from the families who had already squatted
on the vacant lots of this land, the President advised that the
policy in Quezon City should be

> to give preference to people who already have houses on the
> different lots. We should not raffle lots on which a house has
> already been built, unless the owner refuses to meet our
> conditions . . . avoid having to compel people to destroy their
> houses.

By following a humane policy to save individual hardship,
a precedent was set whereby the government gave preferential
treatment to families who had already squatted on government
land.

RECOGNIZING THE URBAN SQUATTER PROBLEM

By 1950, i.e. three years later, the government recognized that
urban squatting and the rapid growth of urban slums were
synonymous, and that a positive programme of action was
needed by the government to prevent the ultimate breakdown
and deterioration of their cities, and as a corollary, a breakdown

---

1. Provision was made in the Charter of the People's Homesite
and Housing Corporation for: "2. (b) the promotion of the
physical, social and economic betterment of the inhabitants
of the cities and populous towns of the Philippines by eliminating
therefrom slums and dwelling places which are unhygienic or
unsanitary and by providing homes at low cost to replace
those which may be so eliminated."

of the high standards of urban life which many had experienced in the Manila of pre-war days. In the same year, the President created a Slum Clearance Committee of nine members under the chairmanship of the Administrator of the Social Welfare Administration (SWA).

Because it was the policy of the government in 1955 to abolish land tenancy in the rural areas (through Republic Act, RA 1400), the Land Tenure Administration also had a role to play in the urban squatter problem. Though the objectives of the Act concerned agrarian land, it was later applied to tenants of large landholdings in urban areas. The government acquired the land in or on the fringes of the city, most of which was already slum, and sold to the occupants just that portion of the slum colony on which their particular shack stood; this transaction, though of good intention, only compounded the problem of slum clearance, making several hundred small urban landowners (each one of whom violated many of the local authority building ordinances) instead of one major landowner with whom the local government could have negotiated for the purpose of acquiring and redeveloping the area.

By a specific Act in 1956 (RA 1597), the government was authorized to subdivide a reclaimed area of foreshore land in the city of Manila, on which several thousand families were already squatting, and to sell to the occupant the land on which each squatter shack was located. Thus not only had the government expressed sympathy for the urban squatters, but the Congress had now openly condoned urban squatting and given protective rights to squatters on government land.

It was not until February 1962 that the Slum Clearance Committee decided that they "should help the squatters from both the private and government lands, and that the Committee should not only transfer the squatters, but should also work out a program to help them progress socio-economically".

The squatter problem in the City of Manila was obviously growing out of all proportion, and in April 1963 the President constituted a Presidential Committee "to study and recommend a solution to the squatter problem", and charged them "to study and recommend measures to deal with the squatter problem on a national scale".

A special inter-agency research and planning team was created. The study team had before them the experience of four previous attempts at relocating urban squatters from the City of Manila.

1951. The first squatter relocation project, at Bago Bantay

A survey of the slums and squatter areas in the city of Manila in 1950 resulted in a count of some 4,300 families within the city limits. Forty hectares in neighbouring Quezon City, known as North Bago Bantay, 8 kilometres from the centre of Manila, and owned by the People's Homesite and Housing Corporation, were set aside for squatter resettlement.

Beginning in 1951, the relocation process was carried out, following in their most literal sense the instructions of the Presidential Memorandum to the Slum Clearance Committee, which were to assist only in the transfer of the families to new sites. The families and the remnants of materials from their shacks were transported by trucks, made available by the City of Manila, to the demarcated lots on the site; there the families were dumped. No provision had been made to assist the families in the erection of their shelters; no roads had been constructed; no water, drainage, or any community rehabilitation facilities had been provided. By 1955, a total of 1,333 families had been relocated on the site, which meant that the relocation site was nearly filled, as it was planned originally to relocate 1,380 families.

After complaints from the resettled families, especially concerning the shortage of water, the Social Welfare Administration provided eight artesian wells and began a programme to encourage the relocated families to construct low-cost sanitation arrangements in the community. Bus companies began to provide regular transport services to and from the city for those who had employment. Up to 30 June 1955, only 591 persons out of 1,333 families were known to have any form of employment, and this was mostly casual labouring only.

Though the Social Welfare Administration (in collaboration with the Quezon City Engineer's Office) allocated a plot to each relocated family, no contractual arrangements were made by the People's Homesite and Housing Corporation for the sale of the plots to the squatter awardees. The families were originally awarded a plot of 75 square metres, but these were later redemarcated and increased by the Corporation to 250 square metres.

Health services, generally, were provided by the Quezon City Health Department, but a new element of support for squatter relocation projects had by this time been introduced: the voluntary assistance of the Bureau of Agricultural Extension and several voluntary charitable institutions, such as World Neighbours, Inc. The settlers were given training by the agencies in projects designed to provide some income, such as hand-sewing, making babies' dresses, paper bags, bamboo fans, weaving mats, laundering, making frypans, breeding tilapia fish, etc., and this programme, undertaken by both government and private agencies, assisted in providing the families with some subsistence.

The second squatter resettlement project, at Bagong Pag-asa (New Hope)

In 1953, as a result of the eviction of a group of squatters from some privately owned land in Quezon City, the People's Homesite and Housing Corporation was requested by the Slum Clearance Committee to make more land available (preferably land adjoining the North Bago Bantay Resettlement Project) for the relocation of these particular evicted squatters. This second project, comprising 652 lots, was known as the Bagong Pag-asa. In this project, the Corporation issued a sale of contract to the occupants as early as 1954, only to find that upon the issue of the contract of sale, many, if not most, of the relocated squatters immediately sold their "rights" to the lots and went back to squatting in Manila, enriched by the experience.[2]

2. A similar reaction was experienced in 1959, when upon a petition from the residents of North Bago Bantay, i.e. the first resettlement project, the People's Homesite and Housing Corporation awarded titles to the occupants of the lots, only to find that the original relocated families sold their "rights" to the land and moved back into other squatter colonies throughout Manila.

1956. Further squatter resettlement projects

In 1956, at the request of the Slum Clearance Committee, the People's Homesite and Housing Corporation made available and subdivided two of the sites totalling 166 hectares at Kamarin, near Novaliches, *25 kilometres from Manila*, for more squatter relocation. This project was demarcated to accommodate 3,542 families on lots of 240 square metres each. The Corporation adopted a policy of requiring the occupants, upon relocation, to enter into sales contracts for the lots, in which clauses pertaining specifically to the non-transference of ownership were provided. The Corporation also began the construction of roadwork from its own funds to assist in making the lots accessible, though no community facilities, such as schools, water supply, drainage, electricity, etc. had been provided by the government for the area.

As a result very few of the relocated squatters stayed on the site, and by 1965 less than 100 families remained, whilst the remainder had returned to live in other squatter colonies throughout Manila; some continued paying their contractual dues to the People's Homesite and Housing Corporation for the purchase of their awarded lots, against the day when public services would be provided. However, of the 3,300 awards, 1,000 were cancelled by the Corporation in 1965 for failure to maintain payment of dues.

Almost exactly the same conditions prevailed in 1966 on the third squatter relocation project, the Gabriel Estate, which had also been opened up in 1956. The estate comprised 32 hectares of People's Homesite and Housing Corporation property, *12 kilometres north of the City of Manila*, and 1,200 lots were demarcated. Again, no funds were provided by the government for the Corporation to construct basic facilities for the relocated families, and as the Corporation, a government agency, received no annual appropriations from the national budget, and as the squatters' incomes were such that little of the capital outlay by the Corporation would be returned, there was a limit as to how much of its own funds the Corporation could afford to disperse on such projects. In 1965, several hundred contracts for the sale of the land to the occupants were cancelled by the Corporation because of non-payment of contract dues, and only a few of the former families still remained on the site.

1960. Sapang Palay

In 1959, many squatter families who had built their shacks in the dried-up river beds and on river banks in Quezon City and other adjoining cities of Manila were caught in severe flash-floods, and many lost their lives. The President, through the Presidential Slum Clearance Committee, provided funds for the People's Homesite and Housing Corporation to purchase the Sapang Palay site of 750 hectares, *37 kilometres north of the City of Manila*, specifically for the resettlement of those squatters from Manila who had been affected, and for others, whose numbers had noticeably increased over the past few years. The selection of the tenants and the relocation of the families in the 1960 transfer of squatters to Sapang Palay were again the responsibility of the Social Welfare Administration, with transport provided by the Armed Forces of the Philippines (AFP).

The government made no specific provision of funds for the development of the site; the People's Homesite and Housing Corporation was expected to provide funds from its normal operational budget for the development of roads, water supply (deep wells), etc., and to find some means of recouping the outlay. Because of lack of employment opportunities or any relatively easy means of subsistence for the families who had been transferred in 1960, less than 600 families had remained on the site up to the end of 1962; 189 were the former occupier tenant-farmers of the site, and some of the remaining families were retired army personnel, for whom a special, though unofficial, provision had been made in 1961. These, through their training, had been able to establish themselves on the land.

Progress of squatter relocation for Manila up to 1963

Up to 1963, 1,668 hectares had been set aside by the government for squatter relocation and resettlement, all of the land being within a 40-kilometre radius of Manila. The area set aside consisted of:

60 hectares in Quezon City (Bago Bantay and Pag-asa), on the fringe of the built-up area of Greater Manila, and 8 kilometres from the centre of Manila, in 1951;

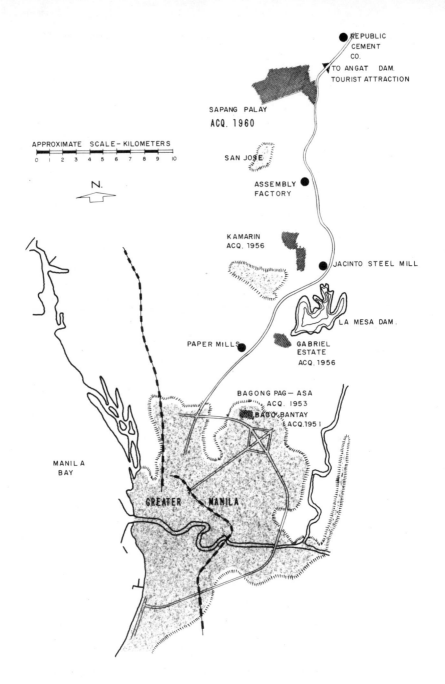

Greater Manila, Philippines
Squatter relocation sites acquired by the Government.

166 hectares which were 25 kilometres north of the city, beyond Novaliches, at Kamarin, in 1956;

32 hectares at Gabriel Estate, in 1956;

750 hectares, which were 37 kilometres north of the city, at Sapang Palay, in 1960; and

660 hectares at sites known as Dasmariñas and Carmona, 25 kilometres south of the city, in 1960.

By 1963, the National Resettlement and Rehabilitation Administration, created in 1958 to establish agricultural resettlement projects throughout the country, had been hampered by lack of capital in seeking to fulfil its objectives; and the Economic Development Corps (EDCOR), established by President Magsaysay in 1950 (when he was Secretary of National Defence) as an agency entrusted with resettling dissident Huks into new agrarian village projects in Mindanao, had been disbanded, although its work had been notably successful.

Quantifying the Urban Squatter Problem

Determining the extent of the problem

The Special Inter-agency Housing Research team (see p. 92), with the full support of all agencies in the government, extended its work to determine the extent of the problem throughout the nation.

The actual relationship of the various categories of squatters, the root causes of migration from rural areas, and the general characteristics and behaviour of the squatter families, their earning capacity, skills, actual incomes, their objectives and aspirations in life, were part of the study.

In March 1963, the actual head count of squatters in Greater Manila revealed a total of 282,730 persons, a figure which, when plotted in relation to the actual head count by the Social Welfare Administration in 1946, of 23,000 persons, in 1956, of 98,000 persons, and in 1963, of 282,730 persons, suggested that there had been a consistently increasing trend of in-migration of squatter families to Greater Manila since 1946. These figures indicated that there had been a constant rate of increase of urban squatters since 1946 at the rate of 15 per

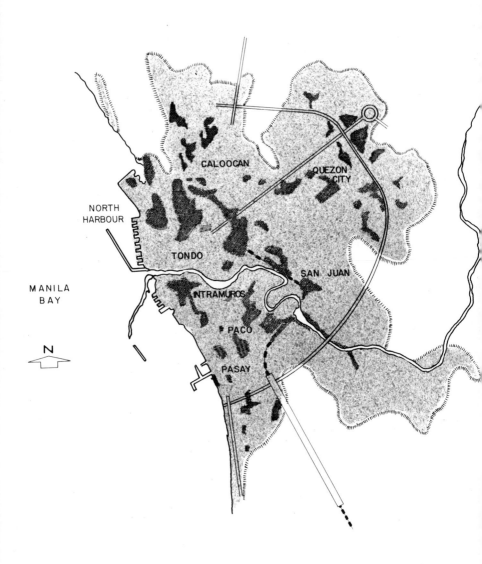

Manila
Urban slum-squatter colonies (May 1963).

cent per annum; if this were to continue unabated over the
next ten years, it could be expected that in 1973 the squatter
population would have increased to approximately 1,300,000,
i.e., 30 per cent of the then estimated population of Greater
Manila; the relationship in 1963 was approximately 10 per
cent of total metropolitan population.[3]

Distribution of squatter colonies in Manila

From air-photo mosaics covering the whole of Greater Manila,
one taken in March 1962, and the other in March 1963, all
the slum and squatter colonies were identified and plotted on
maps; this information provided the basis for the social inter-
viewers in the field to carry out a systematic 10 per cent sample
survey of every squatter colony, and also to identify and
collect information on a wealth of other family characteristics
and circumstances pertaining to the squatters. This was
undertaken by the Social Welfare Administration, with the
help of many volunteers, during the month of March 1963,
and revealed the information which is given in Table D.

The distribution of the slum and squatter colonies throughout
Greater Manila at this time suggested that the colonies were
contained in a wide band, approximately one kilometre in
width, encircling the City of Manila, on a radius of 4 kilometres

---

3. People's Homesite and Housing Corporation, United Nations
   Survey Team, *Metropolitan Manila: Preliminary Report on Housing
   Needs (1963)*. It is significant that a survey carried out in March
   1968, by a special Presidential Committee on Squatter Problems,
   revealed that there were then 127,852 families (767,112 persons)
   living as squatters, and 55,907 families (335,442 persons) living in
   slum conditions, in metropolitan Manila, i.e. a total of 1,102,554
   persons living in slum-squatter conditions. Using the logarithmic
   graph projection (see p. 101), based on the counts of squatters
   in 1946, 1956, and 1963, it was estimated in 1963 that the
   number of persons living in squatter colonies by 1968, if no
   concerted programme of action was implemented, was likely
   to be approximately 600,000. The actual number of 767,112
   squatters suggests an acceleration of the rate of squatter-
   migration into metropolitan Manila.

from the Manila City Hall. This pattern of urban deterioration in a concentric ring encircling the centre of the city is quite a usual occurrence in the expansion process of most cities, for it reflects the growth patterns of the city, and the way in which the in-migratory low-income people invariably settle in the first the instance on the outer fringes of an economically expanding and prosperous city.

Table D. Estimate of slum-dwellers and squatters, Greater Manila, March 1963

	Persons resident in non-squatter slum areas	Persons resident in squatter colonies
Districts of the CITY OF MANILA		
Tondo and San Nicolas	50,000	103,800
Binondo	560	2,230
Caloocan	4,400	14,400
Intramuros	——	22,100
Pandacan	——	9,500
Santa Ana	——	34,000
Sampaloc	7,000	26,000
Santa Cruz	17,340	7,100
Quiapo	——	2,230
San Miguel and Sta. Mesa	200	2,820
Paco	1,540	7,900
Malate	——	18,000
ERMITA	——	1,380
CUBAO	——	14,200
SAN JUAN	——	5,610
MANDALUYONG	——	4,160
PASAY PARANAQUE }	10,700	7,300
TOTALS	91,740	282,730

Urban sociologists sometimes explain this phenomenon on the theory of the cycle of progressive concentric deterioration and reconstruction incurred in city growth. During periods of economic prosperity, there is always a great deal of temporary housing of light construction built on the outer periphery of the prosperous central areas and usually outside the jurisdiction

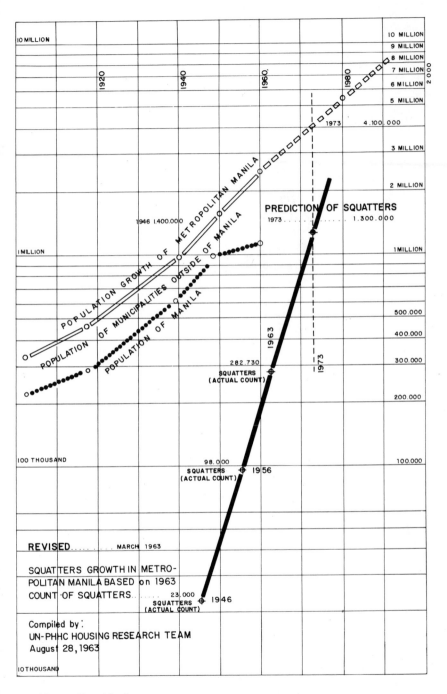

Metropolitan Manila
Projection of growth of squatter population in relation to total city
population growth.

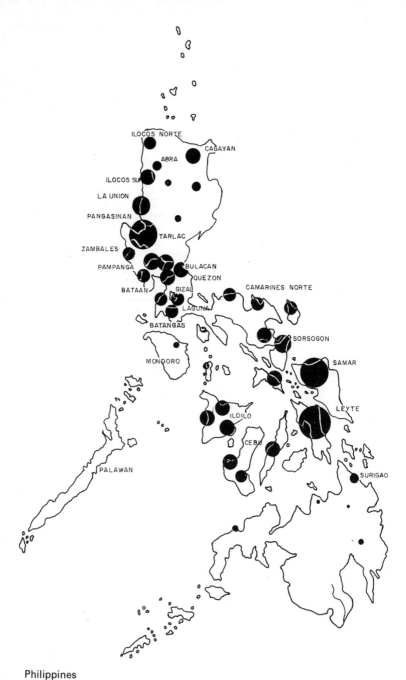

ILOCOS NORTE

CAGAYAN

ABRA

ILOCOS SUR

LA UNION

PANGASINAN

TARLAC

ZAMBALES

PAMPANGA

BULACAN

QUEZON

BATAAN

GIZAL

CAMARINES NORTE

LAGUNA

BATANGAS

SORSOGON

MINDORO

SAMAR

LEYTE

ILOILO

CEBU

PALAWAN

SURIGAO

Philippines
    Proportional origin of squatters to Manila from the various provinces.
    (From house-to-house sample survey, 1963.)

of the local building authority. As the city, over the decades, continues to expand and projects its requirements for further land use beyond the first concentric ring of lower-standard dwellings, the central area of the city, must, of economic necessity, widen its boundaries to include the low-income slum areas which were formerly on the periphery of the built-up area. If the residents of these slum areas have legitimately acquired the title to the land, then, by virtue of the increased value of the land, they are absorbed into and integrated with the urban society. The rebuilding of the originally peripheral slum zone to accommodate the extension of the central area is usually accompanied by a corresponding in-migration of other low-income families from rural areas in search of work, and so large numbers of temporary structures again appear on the outer fringes of the expanding city. The cycle continues over the decades, and in the case of some cities, over the centuries.

By far the greatest number had migrated into Greater Manila from the perennially typhoon-swept provinces of Samar and Leyte, where calamity and famine are an annual occurrence. The second largest group came from the flood-tormented tenant-farm areas of Pangasinan, and the rest, in equal proportions, from the Camarines and Visayas, which are also typhoon-swept zones. Only a few had originated from Mindanao or Cagayan, in Northern Luzon, which are, in fact, major migrant-recipient regions.

The study of the origin of the squatters threw into perspective living conditions in the typhoon belt; the 1960 census revealed that 90,710 of the families resident in the fourteen provinces constituting the typhoon belt were living in *barong-barongs* (makeshift temporary shelters), and these comprised 11 per cent of the shelters in the built-up areas.[4]

The line of minimum subsistence

An important early problem on which the research team needed some quantitative policy decisions was to determine the acceptable levels of living for the families, and to see these levels in relation to an acceptable line of minimum subsistence

4. The typhoon belt includes the provinces of Aklan, Bohol, Capiz, Cebu, Iloilo, Leyte, Marinduque, Masbate, Negros Occidental, Occidental Mindoro, Romblon, Samar, and Sorsogon.

for families throughout the country. A selected group of researchers studied this problem in 1948 and found that practically all consumer commodities, and costs of essential family needs, were always related to the current commercial price of rice, and that all essential factors of consideration for a family budget were measured by the families themselves in terms of the value of a *ganta* (i.e. approximately 2 kilogrammes) of rice. The breakdown of a low-income family budget for a family of four persons was identified as set out in Table E.

Table E. Low-income family budget, 1948

Monthly budget item	Value in rice gantas
Rice	22
Other foods	53
Shelter	16
Clothing	6
Utilities	12
Family advancement, transport, education, recreation, etc.	22
Savings	14
Total	145 units or *gantas* equivalent per month

Assuming some measure of validity in this formula, and adjusting for the needs of (a) a newly married couple and (b) a family of 12 persons (most of whom were reckoned as young children), a graph line representing basic wage or subsistence level at rice costs of P1.10 per *ganta* was plotted against the income scale and the varying number of persons in a family.[5] The survey results, plotted graphically, indicated that the squatter colonies of Manila could be classified as follows:

(a) 81 per cent, or 40,905 families, had an income which provided them with a level of living below the minimum line of subsistence, but above destitution.

(b) 15 per cent, or 7,694 families, were well above subsistence level, and many of those could be considered as belonging to the "speculative" squatter groups:

(c) 1,828 families were destitute and dependent upon Social Welfare (this was verified by the Social Welfare Administration).

[5]. Increased to P1.80 for subsidized rice, in 1966, and P2.20 for commercial rice.

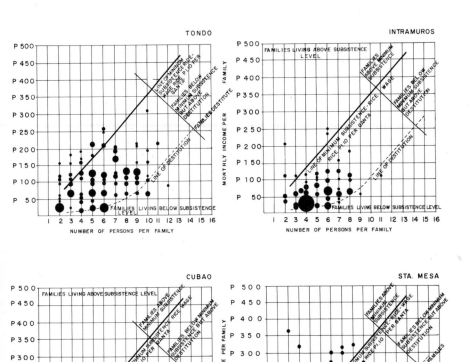

Squatter colonies of Manila
   Survey of family income in relation to family size for four squatter
   colonies. (These graphs are taken from *Urban Squatter Resettlement,
   Sapang Palay—A Case Study in the Philippines* [United Nations Report
   — Restricted], by M. Juppenlatz.)

The report from the Bureau of Census and Statistics, in its Survey of Family Income and Expenditures for 1961, showed that the average annual income for the *urban* casual worker was P1,312 (or P109 per month) compared with P353 (or P29 per month) for the *rural* worker. (N.B.: In 1964, P3.98 = US$1.00, approximately.) This disparity between the income of a slum-squatter in Manila, whose income was established generally as varying between P90 and P180 per month, and the income the same family could obtain if resident in the rural area (always presuming that some kind of employment could be found) is taken to be one of the basic reasons why so many rural families migrate to the cities, i.e. in the hope of improving their standard of living, and particularly that of their children.

The living conditions of the squatters

The conditions in which the squatter families in Greater Manila existed were far below any reasonable standards of urban environmental sanitation, and quite inconsistent with urban living standards generally. The density of the squatter shacks varied, but averaged some 200–400 persons per hectare. The structures were usually a single room, and in the worst squatter colonies hundreds were spaced within a few inches of each other, with no provision for sanitation. On an average, there was one public water faucet serving several hundred families. Obtaining the water supply for the family usually involved waiting in long queues, especially in the dry season, when water was available only for a few hours at night.

In such a form, many of these squatter colonies, because of their lack of hygiene, the bad drainage of their sites, the uncollected refuse, etc., are responsible for the regular (usually annual) outbreaks of cholera in many of the cities. Records from the Medical Intelligence Digest show a high incidence of tuberculosis and respiratory and gastro-intestinal sicknesses[6]

6. Studies carried out amongst the squatter colonies in Singapore revealed a high incidence of the poliomyelitis virus. No equivalent study has been carried out in Manila. See Jan W. L. Kleevens, Lee Liang Hin, "The Occurrence of Enteroviruses in Children from Modern Flats and Squatter Dwellings in Singapore", *Singapore Medical Journal*, Vol, VII, No. 1 (March 1966).

amongst squatter families; these sicknesses are carried to the remainder of the city, imposing a very considerable burden upon the citizens, and also upon the city budget in support of the necessary health and medical services, which are unable to do more than merely maintain a *status quo* of the sickness rates. They cannot eradicate the cause, which remains to inflict the same problems annually.

Some of the squatter colonies were known by the authorities to be the home of organized criminal gangs, the Oxo and Sigue Sigue groups. However, to what extent additional crime originated in the city because of the squatter colonies has not been determined, and the great majority of the families have migrated to the city for self-improvement, not crime. Nevertheless, the authorities asserted that an additional budgetary outlay of P11 million from the city treasury was necessary for extra police services in 1963 to combat the mounting crime wave, while P500,000 annually is budgeted for the care of the juvenile delinquents in the city's jails and institutions.

Suggestions were also made in the local press that much of the damage to buildings from fire, amounting to some P200 million a year, could be attributed to the crime originating in the squatter colonies; but the police subsequently ascribed this to arson by syndicates which were in no way associated with the squatter colonies.

The areas of land selected by the squatters of Greater Manila for their shacks include government foreshore land, properties belonging to local authorities (particularly those which have remained undeveloped), government national parks where there is no evidence of government activity (such as the National Park in Quezon City), swampy lands which are obviously waste land, and increasingly in recent years some private undeveloped lots. There were also some criminal elements who employed armed "goons" to squat on private land with the intention of embarrassing the landowners, in the hope of ultimately being able to obtain actual possession of the land. Fortunately these examples have not been plentiful, but an increase in this tendency was noticed during 1965. Such aspects of urban squatting are not the concern of this book, because there are adequate judicial procedures to which the owners can resort for justice; what does concern us here is the subhuman

Manila
  Typical "hidden" squatter colony, 1966.

conditions under which hundreds of thousands of urban human beings are living at present, and the fact that the numbers of such human beings are increasing at an alarmingly fast rate every year.

The method of social survey adopted for all the squatter colonies of Manila and other cities was to interview the family in every fifth or tenth house, according to the number of field personnel available for survey. Invariably, many university students, secondary school teachers and their senior students, and many volunteer social workers willingly assisted the social welfare agency personnel in carrying out the household survey of squatter colonies. There was a realization amongst many people that the urban squatter problem concerned the population of the entire city.

Squatter colonies in other towns of the Philippines

A question which had to be answered was whether the un-hygienic squalor in which these squatter families were living was the result of the peculiar conditions under which they found themselves upon arrival in Manila, or whether in fact they brought these living conditions with them from their provinces. If the latter, did they aspire to attain a higher urbanized culture and level of living, or were they intent upon retaining their rural habits in their urban squatter colonies as part of their family tradition? The living standards in the squatter colonies of provincial towns and in the rural areas were, almost without exception, low, all with the same characteristics, whether in the typhoon belt area in the Visayas, Mindanao in the south, or Luzon in the north.

It was concluded that if the rural-urban migration could not be checked at its source, then it was becoming a necessity to provide some training for the squatters upon their arrival in the urban areas, and some orientation towards urban living, in order to equip them mentally, technically, and socially for assimilation into the normal urban social and economic scene.

Jolo, Sulu Archipelago, Philippines
   Non-availability of land for housing and lack of security in the hinterland have caused the growth of the squatter colony off-shore. (Photograph taken 1963.)

The characteristics of their architectural and community needs, in accordance with their traditional habits, were studied from the point of view of providing a transitional type of "core house" for a future squatter-rehabilitation and relocation programme.

The excessive density, i.e. more than 600 persons per hectare, in many of the off-shore squatter colonies in the islands of the southern Philippines seems to have been the result of a lack of security on the land, and the extreme difficulty encountered by any of them who tried to purchase land on the periphery of the built-up areas, since all available land was used for growing coconuts, and the owners would not release it. Thus crowding together for group security has now become a habit with many, and it is this habit of living which the squatters have brought with them to the City of Manila. This was indicated by the squatter colonies in the North Harbour, which in 1963 showed a total disregard for providing any space about buildings, even that required for the most elementary community needs. It was, and is still, customary for squatters on the railways tracks to build their shacks within 2 or 3 inches of passing trains; the verges of the railway tracks are crowded with squatter-shacks; and the tracks are used as a playground by the children, despite frequent tragic deaths and accidents.

Although they had voluntarily established themselves in this way, nevertheless a code of behaviour, mutual tolerance, and unwritten rules prevailed (presumably the traditional code of behaviour inherited from their rural *barrios*). This code pertained to the use of what little space was available for drying laundry, to queuing for the water supply, to the storage of their individual cooking fuel, and to other standards of community behaviour.

Diagnostic studies were carried out in twelve other towns and cities throughout the Philippines to determine the characteristics and the distribution of other squatter colonies. The specific studies ranged from the tourist resort of Baguio City, situated in the mountains of northern Luzon, to the town of Jolo, in the Sulu Archipelago in the far south. An inspection of the towns in the Visayas revealed no deviation from the characteristics of squatter colonies in Greater Manila; the standards of accommodation were equally low, but the incomes of the families were, on the average, a little lower.

Manila

Above—The squatter colonies in the North Harbour area. This area was partly cleared in 1963.
Below—Railway line through the North Harbour squatter colony—the playground for the children.

Characteristics under the analysis headings of predominant age group, educational attainment, characteristics of sites (swamps, etc.), provision for sanitation, water supply, prevalence of sickness, and density, *vary* from city to city throughout the Philippines, but the variation is within such tolerably consistent limits that a pattern can be described of the characteristics common to all the squatter colonies throughout the towns and cities of the Philippines at that time.

The results of the survey illustrated that despite the extent of resettlement opportunity and land availability throughout the whole of Mindanao, all cities and towns had a squatter problem, ranging from 7.5 per cent of the population of the developed area of the City of Iligan, to 44 per cent in Marawi, a city some 50 kilometres south of Iligan on Lake Lanao.

It was determined, however, that a good many of the squatters on the shores of Mindanao had originated from the typhoon-swept Visayan Islands, and those in the south of the island had migrated from the islands in the southern archipelago, migrating frequently because of poverty, deprivation, lack of security, and the absence of a sufficient water supply.

COMMON CHARACTERISTICS OF SQUATTERS IN THE PHILIPPINES

Home and family circumstances

Apart from the varying ratio of squatters to urban population, the living conditions of the squatter families in 1963 were tolerably consistent in their poor standard:

(i) *Age.*   The predominant age group in almost all squatter colonies consisted of people below eighteen years of age; the minors comprised more than 60 per cent of the squatter population, compounding the urban problem for the next generation.

(ii) *Educational level.*   The survey indicated that the educational attainments of the squatters were, on an average (though there were variations for each colony), as follows:

Of the heads of household, 30 per cent had received no elementary education;

Those who had received either primary and/or elementary education amounted to 50 per cent; and

Those who had high school or college education amounted to 20 per cent.

(iii) *Overcrowding of families.* Often, in the various squatter colonies, as many as 50 per cent or more of the families were sharing accommodation, frequently a single-roomed shack.

(iv) *Sanitation.* The great majority of squatter shacks in the various colonies had made no provision for sanitation, though, in a small number of squatter colonies, open-pit sanitation was provided by about half the families.

(v) *Water supplies.* Very rarely was there any piped water supply to the dwellings, and in most cases, supply was from a well, pump, spring, or public faucet, often at intervals of more than 100 metres, and usually one faucet for every 100 or 150 families.

(vi) *Sickness.* The incidence of sickness, such as cholera and other gastro-intestinal diseases, pneumonia, tuberculosis, and other respiratory diseases was so high that practically all of the occupants were annually affected by one or more of the above illnesses.

(vii) *Employment.* Approximately 50 per cent of the heads of households had reasonably regular, though casual, work on the wharves or in the markets or the fishing industry; 25 per cent had only occasional, casual employment; approximately 5 per cent were in government or local government services; 20 per cent were unemployed.

(viii) *Densities of settlement.* The densities of the squatter population seemed to average between 300 and 400 persons per hectare, with an exception in Jolo, where it had increased to 680 persons per hectare.

(ix) *Incomes.* The survey revealed that usually, throughout all the colonies, about 80 per cent of the families had an income which provided for less than bare subsistence, 5 per cent were destitute, with the earnings of the remainder ranging from just above subsistence level to a high income.

(x) *Site conditions of colonies.* In practically all cases, more than 50 per cent of the squatters had established themselves in waste swamp areas, on river banks or off-shore in and around the cities, which indicates that, for the most part, they had taken the line of least resistance in the hope of being near enough to the city to gain employment.

The settlement of foreshore and off-shore squatter colonies, which are a feature of all the cities built by the sea, can be observed at its peak in the town of Jolo, in the Sulu Archipelago. It has been traditional to build immediately off-shore; built on the basis of low residential density over tidal water, this type of accommodation throughout all of the hot, humid, tropical climate zones is ideally suited for comfortable living, and helps to adjust the natural environment to "comfort temperatures" without mechanical devices. It is also a most hygienic form of accommodation, for the sea and tide provide a built-in sewage disposal system.

It is a traditional form of housing throughout the southwest Pacific region and some of the tropical zones in South America, particularly on the Amazon River, and it is only to be expected, as the migrants move from island to island towards the centres of greater wealth and opportunity, that they will bring their cultural heritage with them to the cities.

The difficulties of allowing such off-shore squatter colonies to grow in an uncontrolled way, as was the case in Jolo, begin when the colony becomes so consolidated, and so permanent, that the occupants begin to fill in the site under their dwellings in the hope of attaining a title to their "individually reclaimed foreshore lots", causing an obstruction to the normal tidal flow, creating stagnating pools in which are entrapped all waste matter, and causing thereby regular outbreaks of cholera.

Classification of squatters' family types

The classification of the various types of squatter families can be made on the basis of these studies, and, for the most part, can be traced to the provincial heritage and origin of the squatter:

(i) *Foreshore squatters.* There are many whose livelihood has always been from the sea, from fishing, etc., and who have invariably established their colonies on the beaches, rivers, and foreshore lands around the cities; they number approximately 10 per cent of the total squatter population of towns and cities situated in protected areas by the coast.

Frequently with the same group are those who seek shelter from lawless hinterland marauders. The families who have moved in from the rural areas because of the peace-and-order problem of the absence of security, whose whole aptitude directs them towards a rural pursuit, usually possess no skill or training suited for urban living. Upon interview, these families indicated that they would prefer to be resettled in a planned rural community, if given an opportunity.

(ii) *Typhoon disaster families.* These are families who have migrated from the typhoon-swept areas of the Visayas, whose aptitudes are fairly general; they have moved to the city in the hope of obtaining an improved set of circumstances for themselves and their families by turning their efforts to any opportunity in the city which might present itself; they are estimated at about 30 per cent of the total squatters, and more than half of them would wish to continue in agrarian pursuits in an organized community.

(iii) *Economically depressed rural area squatters.* They are families who have left the economically depressed rural areas, where former land-tenancy rulings made it impossible for their families to prosper and develop, and who have agrarian aptitude but are resourceful at turning their hand to any occupation; they are estimated at approximately 30 per cent of total, and the majority of them prefer an agrarian way of life, providing reasonable security of tenure of land is provided.

(iv) *Enterprising families seeking improvement of their own circumstances.* These are families who have received some education in the provincial areas, but, because of limited opportunities to use their education to advance their family circumstances, and owing to the excessively high costs of land or accommodation in various cities, have resorted to squatting in the first instance. They usually take the line of least resistance, and settle in the swamp areas or in lots the occupation of which is likely to cause little objection or resistance from the owners, i.e. the national government or absentee landlords; they number probably about 20 per cent.

(v) *Speculator and professional squatters.* There are, however, still that 10 per cent of the total squatter population who are the speculators and professional squatters, who have tended to give a distorted impression of the whole squatter problem, and who are usually the most forthright in arguing and threatening and talking about their rights as squatters, in the hope of obtaining personal profit and benefit through the misfortunes of others.

By mid-1960, the first generation of children born and bred in these circumstances in Manila are receiving, or have received, a better education in the cities than they could ever possibly have obtained had their parents remained in the economically depressed rural areas. Though the circumstances of their dwelling-environment are not conducive to home-pride and dignity, there is no stigma or indignity amongst the great mass of the population in having one's home amongst the squatter *barong-barongs*, but rather an attitude of tolerant patience towards the national problem and towards the government in particular.

This would tend to suggest that the squatter, as a "collective" citizen of the Philippines, is one with whom the government could readily come to terms and for whom it could formulate and implement effective rehousing and resettlement programmes, knowing that any national investment in such families would be to the national benefit, and would turn their present circumstances, which are a social liability to the towns and cities, into a national economic asset.

An argument which was often presented by many of the urban populace and, therefore, government officials, was that any sympathetic treatment of squatters, in the form of an organized resettlement or rehousing programme, would immediately accelerate an even greater rural-to-urban migration movement, only increasing the number of squatters in the city areas.

The basic reason behind rural-to-urban migration is to obtain improved and reasonable opportunities and circumstances for the family, mostly with the future of the children in mind (for in the Philippines, where the people are predominantly Catholic, the first concern of the parents is the future of the children). Therefore the research team argued that the most rational programme would be for the government to encourage the conversion of this otherwise wasted economic asset, i.e. human labour and family cohesion, into activities of more productive output; to provide the training to enable these people to utilize the natural resources of the land by assisting the under- and un-employed to establish themselves in new, planned, and carefully managed rural and/or agro-industrial communities, located on a planned regional economic distribution, and related specifically to the markets, good-soil areas, trade and commerce centres, and distribution lines throughout the country.

A SQUATTER RELOCATION PLAN

One of the resolutions of the Slum Clearance Committee in 1963 was that an immediate effort should be made to transfer the squatters from Intramuros, Tondo, and North Harbour to the Sapang Palay site in an orderly and properly planned programme of squatter resettlement, and that this project should be treated as a pilot or demonstration project, experimental in the first instance, for the purpose of determining the methods which could be used for extending the programmes to a nation-wide scale of operation.

A technical working group prepared a co-ordinated programme for the selection and transfer of the squatters, and provided a programme aimed at ultimately establishing the families with an economic basis for their community life.

There was, however, a further dilemma to be overcome, and that was in deciding who was going to pay for a squatter relocation project.

Provision is made in the People's Homesite and Housing Corporation Charter for dealing with urban slums, but no appropriations were provided by the government for execution of the programme. The Presidential Slum Clearance Committee was formed in 1950 essentially to locate suitable sites for the placement of dislodged squatters from the city of Manila and suburbs, and finance was provided by the government only for the purchase of the land.

In respect of slum and squatter clearance and resettlement, the People's Homesite and Housing Corporation was in somewhat of a dilemma; the Corporation charter spells out that one of its objectives is to eliminate slums and dwelling-places which are unhygienic or insanitary and to provide low-cost houses to replace those eliminated, but the government did not make any appropriation or working capital available specifically for that purpose.

The human, technical, and economic problems associated with squatter resettlement and rehabilitation were not envisaged when the Act creating the National Housing Commission was drafted in 1940, and, it would seem, were not envisaged in the original Presidential Memorandum creating the Slum Clearance Committee; therefore, adequate provisions for the quite complex procedure which is required have never been spelt out sufficiently specifically in law, and, as the case study of Sapang Palay illustrates, many new complex factors in the operation of such a programme, working both for and against the success of squatter relocation, and invariably concerned with the unpredictability of human nature and personal relationship, have been revealed.

By 7 August 1963, the need for establishing a Squatter Resettlement Agency within the Office of the President, to undertake the responsibility for this project, was recognized by the government.

In view of the difficulty of providing capital for the project, a proposal for interdepartmental collaboration, whereby each department would make its own budgetary provisions for its contribution to the resettlement projects, was drawn up and approved in principle. The requirements would be determined on the basis of an overall development plan and programme. The national priorities for squatter relocation and rehabilitation would first be agreed upon by the interdepartmental representatives in the Agency, and then submitted to the President of the Philippines for endorsement. This procedure was intended to distribute the financial burden of the squatter resettlement project throughout all government departments, and to treat the problems as a national programme of economic and human rehabilitation.

Such a Resettlement Agency had the departmental representation which would have enabled it to engage technically in regional planning and urban development studies concerned with the distribution of population as related to natural resources. In this way, it would have provided an opportunity to deal with the problem of urban squatting by treating its cause, i.e. the economic depression of the rural areas, by planning and developing new resettlement "counter-magnets" in these areas.

The programme envisaged by the working group was to assign a priority to the identified squatter colonies for the action programme, according to the number of families involved in the selected colony, their various family-income levels, and their preference for being transferred to a new community (where the families would be awarded sufficient land for their home subsistence, and would be able to establish their own economic survival, using self-help techniques). An educational programme was to have been carried out among the families, preparatory to their relocation. It was determined that some families wanted to be relocated together, whilst others could be accommodated in low-cost housing projects.

At Sapang Palay, the sites were to be demarcated, water supply distribution system installed, power supply lines connected, elementary and trade schools, market, small industrial estate, health centre, central administration and staff houses built, preparatory to the phased relocation of the families from Manila, commencing with volunteer families for relocation in the early phases.

The sites were to be prepared, with access and the erection of a "core house", which was to be a simple timber frame house, of 9 square metres in area, with *sawali* walls, bamboo slatted floor, and aluminium roofing. The total cost of the house, materials and skilled labour, was estimated at approximately P650 (equivalent to approximately US$162.5).

The families were to be transferred in groups of about 50, and only upon the completion of the core houses; they were then to be organized in self-help groups to enlarge and complete their dwellings, establish their home-economy programme, and construct their own sanitation system. The families were to repay the People's Homesite and Housing Corporation for the land and for the value of materials on an instalment basis, as their family home-economy programme developed over the years.

The economic basis planned for the community was that of an agricultural co-operative, and cottage-type industries. It was estimated that plot size should be between 350 and 500 square metres, according to the land and soil capability of the area. Frontage of each lot was to be 17 metres. Studies were made by agricultural economists on the optimum utilization of the sites, whereby the families could engage in fruit- and vegetable-gardening, poultry- and pig-raising, along the following lines:

Wet season production: Crop-farming of corn, legumes, vegetables, root crops, which should support the proposed feed mill (which in turn, would also draw on waste products from the Rice and Corn Administration and Fisheries Commission), and provide some feed for the livestock throughout the whole project.

Dry season production: Two-layer farming; leafy fruit and bulb vegetation, mushroom-culture on ground-level, with vine vegetation over, which would provide shade, Manure from pig- and poultry-raising projects could be utilized as fertilizer.

Livestock: Each household could have its own small pig-pen, but controlled from a central co-operative for the pig- and poultry-raising projects; the co-operative would be under the guidance of and assisted by the Bureau of Animal Industry, Bureau of Agricultural Extension, and Presidential Assistant on Community Development (PACD), and some of the animal feed, it was hoped, would be available from the United Nations World Food Programme.

Rice: From the 750-hectare property, 200 hectares were to be set aside for irrigated rice fields on a collective co-operative basis.

Employment: The programme of employment over the transition period of resettlement was based on a programme of work involving the preparation of sites, construction of public and community buildings, offices, and houses, and the gradual training of the people in poultry- and pig-raising, mushroom-culture, etc.

It would therefore seem possible to develop an adequate annual income per home; however, a small initial loan would have to be made available, and for this the resources of the National Co-operative Bank were available.

The income which each family could derive from the programme would be directly proportional to the personal efforts
of the family members, and the extent to which the marketing
facilities were involved. It was proposed that the families themselves should constitute the labour force required to build the
new community, with the greater part of the pay for their
labour taking the form of a family ration of food from the
United Nations World Food Programme donations. This,
with a small cash payment, would continue until their own
home-subsistence programme became effective.

The intermediate period of resettlement was expected to be
at least two or three years, until small-scale industrial sites
could be prepared, power and water supply installed, and an
industrial estate established.

The National Agency for the Development of Cottage
Industries (NACIDA) planned to inaugurate training schemes
for the families so that they could engage in small factory work,
homecraft and cottage industries, embracing shoemaking, the
sewing of wearing apparel, tailoring (particularly for the
Philippines Armed Forces), hand-weaving (using abaca fibre,
grown locally), the making of coconut coir matting, carpentry
and furniture making (particularly furniture for government
offices, school desks, etc.), metal craft, and blacksmithing.

The establishment of a central exchange or central co-
operative market, which would be responsible for marketing
and retailing and providing opportunities for employment
through a central organization, and a co-operative banking
system, was envisaged. Some individual credit facilities could
be made available through the NACIDA Bank.

Once the industrial employment programme was under
way, and an earth dam constructed to provide water to
irrigate 200 hectares of rice fields, and the home agricultural
economy was well developed, it was expected that the family
level of income would be above the minimum basic wage, and
could approximate to P3,000 per annum per family (equivalent
to approximately US$750). This would be adequate to ensure
a decent standard of living, and at the same time be sufficient
to amortize repayment for their loans, and provide enough for
some personal advancement and savings. The former squatters
on the land, i.e. those who were working the rice fields before

the actual purchase of the land by the government, claimed for themselves the right to purchase the rice fields, but once the programme of the agricultural co-operative was understood they conceded a preference for membership of the co-operative.

In total, it was envisaged that the programme of development would be the responsibility of a Project Director, whose office would be responsible for the implementation of the programme, and for the administration (which was to lead ultimately to an autonomous local government administered by the people themselves), along with the financial phasing of the master plan: the Project Director would be assisted by representatives from each of the following departments, assigned to the project in the field, each to have his own field office and staff within the central administration building, and each responsible for a specific action programme

Departments	Areas of responsibility
People's Homesite and Housing Corporation (PHHC), Bureau of Public Works	Construction and maintenance staff for infra-structure, security, transportation, and communication.
Home Finance Commission	Home finance guarantee
Co-operatives Administration Office, Philippine National Co-operative Bank.	Co-operative officer and co-operative finance
Bureau of Agricultural Extension, Bureau of Plant Industry	Agriculture, soil and farm management, and supply of seedlings
Bureau of Animal Industry	Livestock and poultry, and supply of breeders and piglets to families
National Cottage Industries Agency (NACIDA) and NA-CIDA Bank	Cottage industry, homecraft industries and credit arrangements
Bureau of Public Schools	Schools and education
Bureau of Rural Health	Health services, doctors, nurses, dentists, and maintenance of health services

Department	Areas of responsibility
Social Welfare Administration (SWA)	Social work
National Water Supply and Sewerage ' Administration (NWSA)	Water supply
Presidential Assistant on Community Development (PACD)	Community development, home-economics programme
National Power Corporation	Power supply

In order to proceed directly with the construction programme, it was requested that Congress appropriate P. 15 million as a capital development fund for Sapang Palay, and the Rice and Corn Administration make some grants of rice, which could be used as a means of subsistence for the families until the United Nations World Food Programme assistance was organized.

It was estimated that the project would take five or six years before a satisfactory financial and community consolidation of the resettled squatters could be expected; however, provision was made for the evaluation of operational progress every six months and readjustment of the programme, as necessary, could then be made.

The programme recommended that if the experiment and experience of the resettlement of the first 50 families proved the plan to be successful, work could commence on the preparation of the additional sites, and the gradual transfer of a further 1,000 families in groups of 50; i.e. a total of 6,000 persons, who should be selected, could commence in the second year as the second experimental stage.

The operational procedure was ready for submission to the government, when, on 2 December 1963, the Mayor of Manila acted on a court authority to "abate the nuisance" of the squatters in Intramuros, Tondo, and North Harbour.

This resulted in 4,500 families (nearly 25,000 people) being deposited on the site at Sapang Palay without any regard to the programme, and with inadequate preparation of the site to receive them. The pilot resettlement project at Sapang Palay had begun — not, however, in the manner in which it was intended.

THE SAPANG PALAY SQUATTER RELOCATION PROJECT — NOT
ACCORDING TO PLAN

The Mayor and his advisers deemed it necessary to clear all
of the urban squatter families in these colonies simultaneously,
on the grounds that

(i) the squatters were so well organized that the prolonged
programme of the Committee would not make any immediate
impact on the squatter problem;

(ii) Intramuros and Tondo squatter colonies were the
breeding grounds of organized crime in Manila, and had to be
cleared immediately;

Intramuros, Manila
  The squatter colonies in 1963. Cleared by the authorities in December
  1963, the area had been cleared previously, in 1960. (Photograph taken
  March 1963.)

Philippines
   Above—Manila. The final "wash", before demolition of their house in the 1963-1964 squatter clearance from North Harbour. (Photograph by United Nations Information Service.)
   Below—Sapang Palay. "Transferring the families at one stage at the rate of 100 per day." A typical relocated family on arrival at the site.

(iii) The operation had to be carried out as a highly concentrated tactical exercise by the authorities, whilst the court
order to "abate the nuisance" was still valid; the Mayor
expected the professional squatters and their legal and legislative
protectors to apply for, and obtain, a restraining order from the
Court within a short space of time. (This, in fact, was exactly
what happened.)

Over the four-month period, from December 1963 to March
1964, 15,000 families, from three of the worst slum-squatter
colonies in the city, were removed before a final restraint-
order from the Courts was imposed upon the local authority.
This action undoubtedly dispersed two of the worst of the
organized criminal elements in the heart of the City of Manila.
Some of the members of the Oxo and Sigue Sigue gangs elected
to be transferred to Sapang Palay, where, under different
circumstances, they revealed themselves as having a different
personal character, that of citizens wanting a chance for their
families to live decently, and an opportunity for regular
employment and a decent life.

Considerable publicity had previously been released through
the press on the development proposals envisaged for Sapang
Palay; it is possible that these press releases encouraged some
of the squatters to transfer to Sapang Palay in the hope of
ultimately obtaining improved family circumstances, in contrast
with their previous experiences.

Calling on the Armed Forces and private hauliers for
transport facilities, the Mayor proceeded to transport many of
the evicted families to Sapang Palay, transferring families at
one stage at the rate of 100 per day.

More than 4,500 families were removed to Sapang Palay
over the period 2 December 1963 to March 1964. The Sapang
Palay project then took on the cloak of a local Mayor-made
emergency, involving 25,000 near-destitute people.

The absence of the full complement of vehicles on the first
few days of the mass transfer of the squatters gave the government a breathing-space within which to marshall their emergency services.

The demolition of the shacks in Intramuros and North
Harbour proceeded efficiently and without any of the violent

reaction from the squatter families which had been predicted by many, following the rumour that an arms factory was known to be in production in the heart of the Intramuros squatter colony. Approximately 25 per cent of the evicted families were transferred to Sapang Palay, whilst the remainder moved to the existing squatter colonies in Quezon City, in particular to the National Park (known as East and North Triangles), and to squatter colonies in Pasay City, contiguous with Manila, while many others swelled the existing squatter colonies which were already scattered throughout the remainder of the City of Manila. A small proportion elected to go back to their province, with assistance provided by the Social Welfare Administration.

The squatter-clearance project of the Mayor was confined to the demolition of squatter shacks on city government and national government property. The ejection of squatters from the adjoining property was finally restrained by a court order because the Land Tenure Administration had acknowledged an appeal from the occupants, and had given an undertaking to the tenant occupants that they would purchase the land at cost and provide the occupants with the title to the site on which they were situated.

Sapang Palay
   The staging and reception area.

Temporary shelter and emergency reception facilities at a
main staging area at Sapang Palay were provided by a volunteer
force from the People's Homesite and Housing Corporation,
the Philippine Constabulary Medical Unit, the Armed Forces
of the Philippines Engineering Construction Corps, and the
Social Welfare Administration teams, and some charitable
organizations. With families arriving at the rate of 100 (or
600 persons) per day, in the first weeks of the emergency, with
little or no physical preparatory work, little water, no sanitation
arrangements, no stores or commercial facilities, the achievement of that band of volunteers can only be termed outstanding
in the service of their fellow men.

They also co-ordinated the voluntary assistance which was
immediately offered by many agencies, both quasi-government
and private, who provided gifts of food, drugs, clothing, and
materials for the families, many of whom were already suffering
from severe malnutrition and much sickness, and had been in
this condition even before their transfer.

A radio-telephone system, connecting the field office at
Sapang Palay with the People's Homesite and Housing Corporation and Armed Forces of the Philippines Headquarters in
Manila, was provided at the outset and maintained by the
Army Signals Corps. This unit did much to solve the all-
important problem of direct communication from the site
(which was 37 kilometres from Manila) during the early
emergency and relocation months. The road connection to
Manila at that time was not good.

The Bureau of Health provided a 5,000-gallon canvas water
tank, the National Water Supply and Sewerage Administration
provided the pump and tapped off their main aqueduct, which
traversed the site, for the supply of water for the staging area.
As many of the families scattered themselves throughout the
750-hectare site, the Armed Forces and Emergency Employment Administration provided the trucks for hauling water
tanks to the various family centres, several times a day.
Seventeen deep wells were brought into operation to add to the
water supply.

By Christmas Day 1963, i.e. in less than three weeks, 1,700
families had been relocated at Sapang Palay — an average
intake of 570 families a week for three weeks. The Social

Sapang Palay
Above—Medical services carried into the field during the early weeks of the relocation of squatters.
Below—"Seventeen deep wells were brought into operation."

Welfare Administration-United Nations International Children's Emergency Fund (SWA-UNICEF) contingent and the office of the Presidential Assistant on Community Development had drawn up their combined programme for action, and this resulted in the organization of the families in residential-block groups, ready to commence self-help housing and community improvement projects.

The National Cottage Industries Agency began a *sawali* (plaited bamboo) training programme, and the trainees were able to use this material as cladding for the walls of their core houses or shelters. Families were given the lumber to build their own core house frames, and the Philippines Armed Forces and the People's Homesite and Housing Corporation provided a carpenter for each group of six families to assist them in the erection of their houses, which were being built according to Corporation plans.

Many private and church charitable organizations, from many different orders of the Catholic and Protestant Churches, responded immediately with offers of assistance, particularly with respect to making available additional food and medical assistance.

The Missionary Sisters of Immaculate Conception had been providing education for the children of the Intramuros squatters and volunteered to continue the teaching programme if a suitable school building or centre could be provided. Many of the volunteer group who cut the bamboo, gathered and laid the *cogon* grass roof, and erected the first school and communal building in this relocation project had previously been members of the notorious criminal gangs, the existence of which constituted one of the reasons for "abating the nuisance" from Manila. The Social Welfare Administration-UNICEF Youth Centre, which had also been serving the squatter families in Intramuros, was transferred to the staging area at Sapang Palay by volunteer efforts and donations.

The Philippine Constabulary Medical Unit, which had contributed invaluable help through the early weeks of the emergency, was followed soon after by volunteer medical personnel from the medical schools at different universities, and the medical team from Operation Brotherhood International (OBI), and WECARE INC. These arrangements

Sapang Palay
Above—*Sawali*-making by the relocated families.
Below—Self-help construction of the "core house" with timber frame
and *sawali*.

Sapang Palay
 Above—The *sawali* house consolidated after twelve months.
 Below—The relocated families begin to settle down.
 Above right—The first Immaculate Conception centre and school, built by volunteer relocated families.
 Below right—A class in progress at the Immaculate Conception school.

Sapang Palay
  The SWA-UNICEF community centre transferred from Intramuros by
  volunteer groups.

satisfied the needs of the settlers for some months until the
Bureau of Rural Health was able to have a proper hospital
and health centre provided.

Though such an emergency does not compare with natural
disasters such as floods an earthquakes, this man-made disaster,
imposed on the government without prior notice, constituted
quite a challenge to the resourcefulness and ingenuity of the
officers of the government and non-government agencies
concerned, particularly as the "natural disaster" fund of the
government could not be tapped, and no previous budgetary
arrangements had been made to deal with such a situation;
there was little in the way of contingency funds available at
the time.

The patience and willingness of the relocated families to co-operate with the authorities, combined with the calm leadership and efforts of those who accepted the responsibility for the task in the field, and the goodwill of so many private charitable organizations and government agencies — all these provided a reservoir of assistance and services which kept the situation reasonably in hand for the first few months of the emergency.

It is much to the credit of the emergency team that none of the members of the relocated families died from illness, epidemics, or exposure, as was the case in the former transfer of squatters in 1960. Several healthy babies were delivered by the Philippine Constabulary Medical Officer in his tented hospital, which was lit only by a hurricane lamp, within the first few days of the resettlement emergency.

The emergency also brought to light an interesting facet of the reaction to such a situation of many of the executive, management officials, and employees of the various government agencies, and volunteers from the non-government agencies. These people put aside all their 8 a.m. – 5 p.m. working rules, and their status and rank, and worked hard and long, helping the work in the field, often far into the night (by the light of the truck head-lamps), in order to prepare the staging areas and temporary shelters and facilities, and assist those families who had no shelter or who had been doubling up with other families in Manila or whose shelters were totally wrecked beyond the possibility of salvage, in the demolition process.

When the initial emergency had been resolved, i.e. by the end of February 1964, the next problem was to maintain and support the families until the administration could marshall its resources and finances and assist them to organize themselves on a self-supporting basis. Though plans had been drawn up for this transition-employment stage, it proved to be the most critical stage in the whole undertaking, for the relocated families had come out of the shock of the hurried transfer and were expecting some energetic follow-up action by the government for their economic support and livelihood. A list of the employment-aptitudes of 2,557 heads of household, who were transferred, indicated a large work force which, if integrated in a community construction programme, could contribute to the establishment of a balanced new community (see Table F).

.

Sapang Palay
The Health Centre subsequently completed.

Table F. Squatter families—Employment aptitudes or skills of the relocated families revealed in interviews over the period 1 December 1963 to 28 February 1964

Kind of employment in which squatter was previously engaged	Number of heads of household
Baker	6
Barber	23
Beautician	4
Butcher	3
Caddy	9
Carpenter	142
Checker	5
Cook	23
Dressmaker, tailor	73
Driver	154
Electrician	17
Employee	104
Engineer	5
Farmer	5
Fisherman	37
Foreman	4
Home industry and pig-raising, umbrella repairer, watch repairer, shoe repairer, handicraft worker, paper-bag maker, poultry raiser, shoemaker, rubber-stamp maker, woodcraft worker, embroiderer	33

Janitor, messenger	22
Journalist	1
Labourer, stevedore, helper, waiter, baby-sitter, waitress	1,106
Laundry man, laundry woman	106
Lawyer	1
Mason	21
Mechanic	32
Midwife	3
Operator	11
Optometrist	1
Painter	36
Pensioner	2
Photographer	3
Plumber	5
Policeman	2
Quartermaster, captain of a motorboat, seaman	48
Salesman, salesgirl, agent, storekeeper	48
Scavenger	7
Security guard	70
Shoe shiner, newspaper boy, washboy, polisher	20
Soldier	3
Stage actress	1
Technician	6
Tinsmith, vulcanizer, welder, blacksmith	17
Tutor	4
Vendor, merchant, fish dealer, buying and selling, sari-sari store, RCA retailer, pedlar	334
Total	2,557

There is no substitute in life for the basic means of family subsistence. The people knew that much was being done by the government to help them, but the level of organization required under these circumstances proved beyond the capacity of the government at the time, and the unemployment problem was not solved by the end of March 1964. As a result, the relocated families became hungry and restless for some action towards their economic survival.

The organizational capacity required to convert the various proposals of the development plan into the very complex co-ordinated inter-agency programme of action in the field was putting the government to a real test. Meanwhile, the emergency team, assisted by many volunteer personnel and agencies, kept a programme of health and food and home economy going.

But the long-range programme required that considerable finance be made available immediately by the government, for the construction of public buildings, the infrastructure, and to support the labour force; this was simply not available.

Sapang Palay — The Relocation Programme Takes Shape

However, by the end of 1965, as a result of the consistent efforts of the government and non-government agencies, the Sapang Palay project had been successfully reoriented and reactivated into the pilot squatter-resettlement project, as originally envisaged by the Presidential Slum Clearance Committee. By this date, only 2,820 families (nearly 17,000 people) were registered as remaining in residence in Sapang Palay, compared with the 3,415 families who were registered as having been resident in the project in August 1964, and the total of 5,975 families who had been registered as having been admitted to the project since 1960.

Much had been achieved, considering that government support for the programme had been mostly in personal effort, unsupported by financial releases. The Presidential Assistant on Community Development, the Social Welfare Administration-UNICEF contingent, and Operation Brotherhood International had, between them, direct contact with all the families; all of the families had been allotted a permanent site, and all had been organized into recognizable "block" and *barangay* groups (the latter of which contained approximately 25 families), each under a block leader, or a *barangay* leader. Prior to the 1963 relocation there already existed the Council of the former tenants, with the *Barrio* Captains, and there was now an amicable blending of the interests of the former tenants and the resettled families. Through this line of communication, the families were being kept fully informed about the development programmes of both the non-government and the government agencies, and at the same time, the views and problems of the various groups were being conveyed to the government for action. The families were also organized for community self-help projects.

In the field, i.e. on the Sapang Palay site, an Inter-Agency Co-ordinating and Development Council had been formed

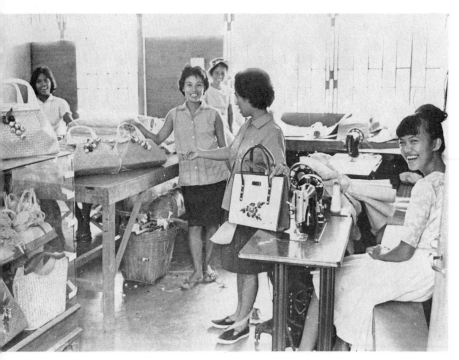

Sapang Palay
Craft-work training at the Operation Brotherhood International Centre.

from amongst all the agencies working in Sapang Palay, and this was governed by its own articles of organization.

This Council promises to be the most satisfactory administrative unit for co-ordinating and prescribing the implementation programme at Sapang Palay; the *barangay* groups and *Barrio* Captains are represented, and it is possible to concede that this Council can ultimately assume the role of the local government instrumentality for Sapang Palay; as the economy of the community develops and becomes more self-sufficient, so more authority can be allocated to the Council, until ultimately it becomes the constitutionally recognized local authority for the area.

The Bureau of Public Highways had provided a good concrete road surface from Manila to within 4 kilometres of Sapang Palay; a new heavy-duty reinforced concrete bridge across the river en route was completed; work had commenced on the completion of the reinforced concrete road to cover the last 4 kilometres.

Fast buses to Manila traversed the area at half-hourly intervals, taking approximately one hour from Sapang Palay to the centre of Manila.

A 200,000-gallon reinforced concrete reservoir had also been completed along with several kilometres of main 4-inch and 6-inch water distribution lines, with upstand pipes and faucets every 100 metres.

At the time of writing, negotiations with the Electricity Authority were well advanced for the installation of a 1,000-kw sub-station.

A small industrial estate of 20 hectares, adjacent to the sub-station and the main water aqueduct, the main highway and the river, is now being developed with the roads, drainage, and site development, for sale or lease to industrialists for the purpose of establishing labour intensive industries. Industrial plants envisaged at present range from a small steel and wire drawing plant to a factory for making furniture and prefabricated building components, and a food cannery.

Adjacent to the industrial estate, a site is reserved for the construction of a Technical Training Institute, to embrace training in all forms of trade, and electrical and mechanical skills, for it is envisaged that this should be a regional institute for the training of selected squatter families in "cadres" of the various skills required for moving into new areas of land and preparing the area for the transfer of more urban-squatter families. As the present negotiations proceed to a successful conclusion, it is envisaged that the Sapang Palay Institute will in fact be the training centre in the Philippines for the team leaders of future squatter-resettlement projects, who will be selected for those projects from among the urban squatters themselves.

No arrangements have been made yet for the award of titles to the occupants, as such an action has many consequences, some of which could be detrimental to the overall programme. However, the families are assured of security of tenure of their lot whilst they remain in occupation. A programme of self-help housing was being worked out through the "block" and barangay groups, with the assurance of an award of title after ten years' residency on site.

On 18 July 1966, Republic Act 4852 was made law by the

President. This Act provided that a National Centre was to be established at Sapang Palay "to study and devise solutions to the problems of urban squatting and/or for the training, relocation and rehabilitation of urban squatters". Provision was made in this Act for adequate finance for the training programme and centre.

THE CENTRAL INSTITUTE FOR THE TRAINING AND RELOCATION OF URBAN SQUATTERS (CITRUS)

This Research and Training Centre was intended to satisfy the needs of the families resident in Sapang Palay, and also to serve as the orientation and training centre for a greatly enlarged programme of urban squatter selection and relocation into a pattern of new agrarian communities.

There is still much experimental and scientific work to be undertaken before a large-scale working programme for the relocation of existing urban squatters and the deflection of the rural-to-urban migratory families into a new settlement pattern can be accomplished.

Already, sufficient research has been carried out by the various academic and scientific agencies concerned with the settlement-supporting capacity of the land and the social organization of the rural and agrarian society to begin cautiously extending the programme of planned settlements in relation to the metropolitan area.

The basic sense of values and communal structure within the growth pattern of agrarian towns evolving into urban centres throughout the Philippines has been established by various studies, most notable of which is the work of Mr. Isao Fujiuroto, who has been able to apply a scale analysis to the cultural evolution of a group of towns and cities in Mindoro. This study reveals the typical sequence by which communities evolve to greater participation in the national social structure.

This knowledge can now be applied within the context of a programme for the relocation of families into self-help communities, and for the accelerated upgrading of the manpower capacity of selected urban squatters prior to their relocation. The communities need to have a spatial relationship within the regional economic development context, and the population-supporting capacity of the land. It is now possible to plot a programme for harmonizing the social evolution of the squatter and his family to maintain family and community cohesion (essential to sustain the economic growth of the community) within a community growth pattern, within which the human resources of the families themselves constitute the real source of wealth for the community.

Surplus manpower is available in abundance in the urban squatter colonies; the territory for resettlement is available; the pressure of population is now making the great metropolis burst at the seams, socially and economically. Needed now are the organizational capacity, leadership, and pre-investment capital to support the urban-to-rural migration programme and to retain more of the rural families in the hinterland.

In 1966, it was envisaged that the Central Institute for the Training and Relocation of Urban Squatters at Sapang Palay would comprise five main training centres:

  (i) The Human Resources Training Centre
 (ii) Manpower Services and Vocational Training Centre
(iii) Agricultural Co-operative Demonstration Centre
 (iv) Settlement Research and Programming Centre
  (v) The Joint Inter-Agency Administration Centre

There are, as yet, many unpredictable reactions and facets to the problem of systematically relocating urban slum squatters into new communities within a planned pattern of new settlements. The following are but a few of the many facets of the programme (and problem) on which serious research work, carried out on a scientifically controlled method, needs to be undertaken:

the methods of selecting families who are temperamentally suited for relocation;

the process of developing their human resources and manpower through an organized and controlled training programme in order to accelerate their productivity and, at the same time, retain their family cohesion and social harmony; the development of incentive techniques for utilizing the manpower of the relocated families in the physical construction of a large segment of their new communities;

the economic programme for generating wealth from the natural resources of the new resettlement sites and provision of the regional infrastructure in such a way that the communities will perpetually contribute to their own subsistence and the gross capital formation of the country.

It is from the results of such scientifically controlled social, economic, and physical development studies that reliable methods for extending the urban squatter relocation programme on a nation-wide scale can be planned and integrated with the national economic development programme. The results of the same studies will, in all probability, be applicable to the problems of many countries, and therefore will be extremely valuable from an international point of view.

The subject matter proposed for the training and work of each centre was as follows:

Human Resources Training Centre
Training programme

Personal and family	Home and lot	
	Indoor	Outdoor
Family budgeting	Furnishings	Self-help housing
Beauty culture	Hygiene and comfort	Garden productivity
Kitchen economy	Household utensils	Animal husbandry
Nutrition	Kitchen economy,	(piggery and
Hygiene and	preserves, etc.	poultry)
sanitation	Accident prevention	Garden drainage
Family cohesion	Homecraft	Waste disposal
Recreation	textile making	Sanitation
Literacy	pottery	Environmental
Personal skills	woodwork	sanitation
	bamboo and rattan	Fish culture
	light assembly	

Community development	
Block	Community
Group organization	*Barrio* Council administration
Group representation	Adult education for literacy
Barrio aggaris	Hospital and health services

Block	Community
Mutual assistance for essential services, e.g. water social services youth group activities child welfare mother care self-help housing credit union industrial craft consumer co-operative nursing care for aged recreational activity education for children *barrio* laws and regulations	Local government administration parks and gardens maintenance refuse collection and disposal community tidiness security and police services transport services communication Banking and savings Credit unions Consumer co-operatives Self-help community construction District sports Cultural centre Higher education Community action Puericulture Community and national law and legislation The constitutional rights of the individual Labour and manpower and law Industrial activities

The Human Resources Centre also has a role to play in the total programme, and would be responsible for:

Administration of the Transient Station
Training programme and discipline
Accommodation and food
Sanitation and recreation
Relocation of the families into new communities.

Manpower Services and Vocational Training Centre
(in collaboration with Department of Labour and Bureau of Vocational Education)

Apprenticeship	Manpower and vocational training programme	Labour extension services
Aptitude testing	Draftsmanship architectural machine shop graphic arts	Occupational opportunities
Basic education		
Language and grammar		Direction of skilled
General science	Machining and lathes	manpower

Apprenticeship	Manpower and vocational training programme	Labour extension services

Mathematics
Labour laws and regulations
Industrial laws
Elementary economics of production and labour
Office methods
Accident prevention
	Foundry work and casting
	Pattern making
	Sheet metal working
	Welding
	Electrical
	  power
	  electronics
	Mechanical
	  automotive
	  maintenance
	  machinery
	Ceramics
	  block-making
	  pottery
	  kilning
	Building trades
	  carpentry
	  joinery
	  masonry and paving
	  concreting
	  steel working and bending
	  glazing
	  plumbing and drainage
	Leathercraft
	Painting, binding, and stationery
	Photography
		Small-scale industries promotion
		Industrial estate development
		Marketing of products
		Labour counselling

Agricultural Co-operative Demonstration Centre

Leadership training	Productivity	Canning distribution and marketing
Co-operative management Accounting and auditing Labour relations Consumer co-operatives Credit unions Banking procedures The economics of agricultural production	Soil quality and fertilizers Soil husbandry Animal husbandry Selectivity of crops and seeds Plot management Irrigation control	Factory management and labour relations Food technology Equipment engineering preparation processing packaging storing

Leadership training	Productivity	Canning distribution and marketing
Procurement procedures Security systems	Equipment maintenance Slaughtering — rules and regulations Storage procedures and methods Preservation of commodities	Accounting and auditing Market operations Economics of transport and delivery Marketing economics and market price indicators

Settlement Research and Programming Centre

Improved patterns of human settlement through a programme of social and economic adjustment

Research unit	Regional and physical development unit	Logistical support unit for new settlement and local project
Methods of selecting families for relocation Methods of selecting employment aptitude Manpower utilization programme Evaluation of reaction and response of families to programme Evaluation of resettlement techniques Evaluation of training programme Building technology for low-cost construction Sanitation and environmental hygiene Soil utilization for nutritional needs Family survival methods in undeveloped regions Legal problems of urban squatting	Analysis of economic and resettlement potential of regions Central area redevelopment Urban diagnosis Selection of sites for new communities Regional infrastructure development programme Layout of new communities Local infrastructure programme Economic development programme Logistical support programme for relocation	Acquisition of land Subdivision of land Water supply section Power supply section Road construction team Building construction team Medical team Stores and procurement office Transport and equipment pool Security team Waste and refuse disposal Emergency and commercial food supply Agronomists and soil husbandry Animal husbandry Communications

Joint Inter-Agency Administration Centre

Responsible for local operations — local administration at Sapang Palay

Local operations	Social and economic rehabilitation
Master plan implementation	Social services
Infrastructure, construction of roads, drainage, buildings, etc.	mother care
	child care
Subdivision and award of contracts for lots	youth clubs
	nutritional safeguards
	home industries
Schools and education programme	self-help housing
	mutual aid in community development
Administration of shopping and marketing centres	credit unions
	co-operative consumer
Security and police duties	garden economics and productivity
Health and medical services	
Transport and equipment pool	labour and employment service
Health and sanitation services	recreations and amusement
Communication	
Reafforestation	
Water supply	
Power supply	
Industrial estates	
Barrio Council and local government representation	
Barrio Council private agency participation	

PART TWO

Urban Squatting in Perspective

"It is surely of the very essence of the evolution concept — hard though it be to realize it, more difficult still to apply it — that it should not only inquire how this of today may have come out of that of yesterday, but be foreseeing and preparing for what the morrow is even now, in its turn, bringing towards birth."

Sir Patrick Geddes
Cities in Evolution

CHAPTER FOUR

Urban Squatting in Its Historical Context

THE CITY: AN HISTORIC REFUGE OR AN INSTRUMENT FOR THE CREATION OF WEALTH

In the progressive stages of a nation's urbanization process the city is a culminating point and usually expresses in its total character the level of advancement to which that society has evolved, and the organizational capacity of the society of that city at the time of enquiry. The city has appeared many times throughout the past; in the history of the Chaldees, of Egypt, of Ancient Greece, during the time of the Roman Empire, under the tutelage of the various monarchies of the Middle Ages, in Europe, the Middle East, India and the Far East, and in Central America, there is a mass of evidence demonstrating the various phases and advances made in city building and in the urbanization process, and indicating the emerging strength of society at that time in history. However, not all cities have survived as living organic structures. Their "skeletons" are still being unearthed by archaeologists today, and it is from these remains that much is being revealed about the living standards of the societies which occupied those cities, their concepts of the use of space, planning, organizational and technological ability, their rituals, beliefs, sense of taste and decoration, their commercial activities, and way of life.

There is no denying the necessity for using the example of our past history as the source from which to draw stimulus for the laying of plans for the future, and in this sense we need to explore the origin of our cities. Any attempt, however, to project the existence of urbanized societies, as expressed by cities, beyond recorded history, can only be conjecture, though Plato, in his *Timaeus*, would have us understand that the most highly evolved of all, the famed city of Atlantis, existed some 15,000 years ago. (Legend has it that by 9000 B.C. Atlantis, many leagues beyond the Pillars of Hercules, was overtaken by a cataclysm and totally submerged. However, an interesting interpretation of Timaeus-Critias by Professor J.V. Luce, in his volume, *The End of Atlantis*, may prove that the legend has previously been misinterpreted.)

The most reliable evidence we have of the existence of cities in our pre-history era is to be found in the "fertile crescent" of the Tigris-Euphrates river basin. Great cities, built by organized groups under priest-kings, cities whose remains indicate a high level of social, economic, and organizational capacity, were in existence during the neolithic era.

Though the archaeological work of Dr. Kathleen Kenyon indicates a comparatively sophisticated city at Jericho in approximately 8000 B.C., most of the evidence is generally dated after the time of "the flood". Sir Leonard Woolley, with many other great scholars, conjectured that "the flood", referred to in Genesis 7:17, was actually the inundation of the Tigris-Euphrates River basin and the inundation of the cultured societies contained therein. Archaeologists, digging in and around the site of Ur of the Chaldees, have revealed a band of clay, approximately ten feet thick,[1] overlying the whole district. Taking into account other evidence, such as the existence of settlement below the band of clay, these archaeologists assert that a great flood certainly overtook the district in or around 4000 B.C. If there were advanced urbanized settlements or city states in this district in the era prior to "the flood", the evidence has been obliterated, and therefore, from the evidence available, we date the city, as an expression of the collective abode of organized society, from circa 3500

[1.] Werner Keller, *The Bible as History*, trans. W. Neil (London: Hodder and Stoughton, 1956), pp. 48–50. Illustrated

B.C.[2] Within the remains of these cities, much was found to indicate the language of their inhabitants, their system of writing, arithmetic, trade and commerce, civic laws, codes of behaviour, etc., and, in principle, these ways and customs bear a striking resemblance to many of the ways and customs in various parts of the world today.

During the time of our recorded history, man and his family have lived in various stages of social and economic organization, usually interdependent, within either:

(i) organized, disciplined towns and communities, or commercial ports, many of which persisted up to less than a century ago as walled towns;
(ii) in established agrarian or forest communities (including fishing villages), producing food both for themselves and the town market; or
(iii) in nomadic pastoral groups, which, apart from living off the land, often provided the meat and the quadruped mobility for the society and traders of the day.

There is a transitional group embracing the miners, quarry workers, and hunters, which, for the purpose of this reference, can be classified as belonging to the nomadic group.

The pattern of this settlement (or the physical location of these three groups) was by no means always static; the changes in the pattern of settlement, which was invariably based on their social cohesion and the economics of survival, were governed by the natural elements, and factors of economic geography and social history. Throughout history, erosion, or change of climate, often forced a change in the physical location of the agrarian communities; plunder and blood feuds often left handsome walled cities as piles of smouldering rubble.

Just as there were frequent changes in the physical location of the three groups, so there was also an interchange within the social order (or levels) of people and families both within and between the three groups.

There has always been a recognizable movement of people from the land and agrarian pursuits towards the towns and

2. Gideon Sjoberg, "The Origin and Evolution of Cities", *Scientific American*, September 1965, pp. 55–74.

between the towns, usually from the smaller to the larger towns; sometimes the city has been used as a place of refuge, but also, invariably, the move has been made in quest of more trade and commerce, work or opportunities for self-improvement, and in the hope of increasing and accumulating personal wealth. This is outlined clearly in the principle of "geographic control" propounded by Sir Patrick Geddes, in describing the Valley Section.[3]

There have been long periods in history when the city has been regarded as a place of refuge, particularly against marauders or invaders. The motivation for the drift from rural or agrarian pursuits to town-life can be described as twofold, for personal advancement and for the sense of security, sometimes only the psychological sense of social security, which the city accords.

It can be argued that, given the explosive overall increase in population of the underdeveloped countries (see Estimates of World Population Increase, Tables A, B, and C, and diagrams relating to these tables in chapter 1), and the low per capita earning capacity which the land provides, if the rural population is not to continue to increase excessively, thereby causing a reduction in the per capita income of the rural population to an even lower level than at present (as is adequately demonstrated in Latin American countries),[4] then rural-to-urban migration must be expected to increase.

While rural development and agricultural policies of governments of developing nations may reduce, they will never eliminate, this migration trend, which can be described as a mass descent of people upon the cities in the developing nations.

The rate of rural-to-urban migration for both the developed and developing nations has apparently been much the same over the past century as it has been over the past thousand years.[5] The reason for the actual increase in city population

3. Sir Patrick Geddes, *Cities in Evolution* (London: Williams and Norgate), p. 1.
4. United Nations, *World Social Situation* (1963) (New York: 1963). See section on Latin America.
5. C. M. Cipolla, *Economic History of World Population* ("Pelican" [Harmondsworth, Middlesex: Penguin]), pp. 75–105.

can be found in the change in the death rate in the city, for child mortality has been reduced, life expectancy has been extended, and the actual birth rate in urban centres has increased. In Europe, for example, the birth rate has been higher in the rural areas, over the past several hundred years, than in the towns or cities. This is also true for the developing nations today. [6]

Over the past thousand years, the disciplines governing the distribution of and dominion over territory, the use of land, the control of population throughout the land, and the form of government (or the form of social contract of the people with their king) have undergone considerable change.

For the most part, the inhabitants of twentieth-century towns and cities, expecially those of the less developed nations, reside under a different form of social contract, and a different form of global economic concept, from those obtaining in the cities of Europe, or the Orient, at the turn of the last millennium.

Some of the metropolitan centres of today have grown from the remnants of city states, but on the whole the urbanized structure of the world of the twentieth century derives predominantly from the concept of global trade and commerce patterns which have emerged over the past 300 years, intensified over the past 150 years with the creation of intensively industrialized cities, all of which can survive only by being able to feed on bigger and increasing "market pastures" for their products.

To some extent, it was probably a combination of the pressure of population on the cities (recognizable in its own content

6. It is demonstrated in *World Population Prospects, As Assessed in 1963* (United Nations, Department of Economic and Social Affairs, Population Studies, No. 41), pp. 3 and 4, that "mortality has recently declined tremendously in some developing countries but less in others. In developed countries, on the other hand, the mortality level is now low and the range of variation is rather small. The great majority of developing countries is included in a range of expectation of life at birth from about 30 to 60 years. A similar majority of developed countries is represented by a variation in expectation of life from about 67 to 77 years."
"In nearly all of the developing countries, there remains considerable scope for rapid decreases in the death rate, so that the prevailing tendency is one of accelerating population growth."

in those days), and the need for more wealth to achieve higher living standards for the city, which led to the ambition of the several establishments of Europe for more wealth. Wealth was conceded to be derived from dominion over territory, and this, no doubt, contributed to the agreement between the Kings of Spain and Portugal in 1494, when, by the treaty of Tordesilhas, they divided the territory of the world between them, along meridian 50°W and 130°E.[7]

In the northern latitudes of Europe it may have been the harsh climate which caused people to regard the shelter of the city with such significance. Then, as a result of the growing pressure of population within the confining city walls, the city-dwellers were probably stimulated towards economic expansion in quest of a life of greater comfort and convenience (or they were responding to the challenge of their environment, as Arnold Toynbee demonstrated[8]). But when the same hypothesis is applied in the case of the less developed nations, most of which are in sub-tropical lands, the *environmental factor of climate* obviously cannot be considered as contributing to the stimulation of economic expansion, since here very little is required in the way of solidly constructed shelters for comfortable survival. Here the only marauder of the plains from which the peasants flee is poverty and lack of security.

Perhaps it was the recognition that literacy, accounting skills, geographical knowledge, etc., could provide the means of reaching higher living standards that spurred the members of society of the day into secular education. This was made possible by the established church which had kept literacy alive and so provided the foundation from which the new education developed.

7. Arthur Davies, *Geographical Journal* (Royal Geographical Society, London), CXXXIII, Part 3 (September 1967), 337.

8. Arnold Joseph Toynbee, *A Study of History* (abridged version, abridged by D.C. Somervell [London: Oxford University Press, 1963].
The principal thesis of Professor Toynbee is that societies or civilizations (not nations or periods) are the significant units of historical study. Civilizations, twenty-six of which were distinguished, including arrested societies, grow by responding successfully to challenges under the leadership of creative minorities; they decline when the leaders fail to respond creatively. (*Encyclopaedia Britannica* (1961 edn.), XXII, 337.)

However, whatever might be the motivating factor, or combination of influences, Europe emerged from the Dark Ages as an economically and socially orientated group of nations; trade and commerce began to flourish and extend over larger areas; the spread of literacy increased, skills were patronized, and wealth was being created from craft, inventiveness, and the ingenuity of people living within an organized social discipline; there was a growing recognition that wealth could be created by means other than dominion over, and the product and value of land. It was being created from the skill and productivity of the human resources of the towns, to meet the markets provided by the needs of society of the day and their own rapidly accumulating wealth. It was being created by the extension of trade and commerce, and new financial systems were being innovated, based on credit, guarantees, and the provision of capital to foreign enterprises for the purpose of generating more capital.

The culmination of this evolutionary process can be seen in the emergence of several maritime cities in Europe, such as Antwerp, Bruges, Lyons, Genoa, and Venice, in the seventeenth century, as centres for shipping, trade finance, and sources of capital for long-term financing on an international scale. Amsterdam and the City of London became the two principal international centres during the eighteenth century, and institutions were established in these cities which laid the basis, and the financial system for the extension of trade and commerce on a global scale — their activities covered such matters as money to finance goods which never touched the shores of Europe, insurance against risks anywhere in the world, foreign transactions in gold, arbitrage in foreign securities, and the chartering of ships from and to any port in the world.

The emergence of a global financial system was a reflection of the age. Trade and industry were developing rapidly, new industrial processes were emerging, and savings were beginning to accumulate in commercial hands. Joint stock companies were starting to develop. The Dutch East India Company, established in 1602, is believed to have been the first joint stock company in the world. [9]

9. William M. Clarke, *The City in the World Economy* ("Pelican" [Harmondsworth, Middlesex: Penguin]), pp. 15–23.

With the expansion of financial activities, and with the cities of Europe now having the means to market their products more widely throughout the world, some of the leaders of society began to recognize the need to safeguard the health and welfare of the city residents, and from this there gradually evolved an effective local government system.

One maxim has emerged clearly from the evidence available, and that is that over this period the rate of urbanization in European and American cities bore a direct relationship to their rate of economic growth. The urbanization process of the developing nations is very different. Here the population growth trend of the cities is for the most part in excess of their economic growth rate. The economic expansion of northern hemisphere cities in the eighteenth and nineteenth centuries was considerably dependent on industrialization, which, once set in motion with the aid of machines, must have markets, markets, and more markets, all with a purchasing power, to keep the industrial machines in operation and the city population employed. Most of the developing nations have emerged from the colonization policy of foreign lands — a policy which was conceived to provide for the future expansion of the "machine" economy of Europe; many of the countries became the essential source of raw materials for the home industries. Colonization of underdeveloped territory was already an established policy of European countries before the eighteenth century.

However, the time came when the individual systems for creating wealth (through an industrial economy, dependent upon a large international pattern of trade and commerce) had to be protected; conflicts, challenges, and war between the several highly organized societies of Europe, each with its own colonial possessions, grew in intensity; a large segment of the accumulated capital and wealth was set aside for defence and security, and for protecting commercial interests and the system. The conflicts came to a climax in the 1939–1945 world war, when many countries engaged in the fight came to the realization that what was at stake was the basic principle of the liberty and survival of the rights of the individual of future society.

Even before the cessation of hostilities, on 25 April 1945

the governments of China, U.S.S.R., Great Britain, and U.S.A. convened an international conference to draw up a charter for a United Nations' Organization. By 24 October 1945, with 46 member-nation signatories, the charter came into force. The primary objective was the maintenance of international peace and security, but equally important in the charter was the objective of the development of friendly international relations, based on the principle of equal rights and self-determination of peoples, and the achievement of international co-operation in solving international problems of an economic, social, cultural, or humanitarian character. There were 126 member nations in 1967.

Through the principle of self-determination adopted by the United Nations, many former colonial countries adopted self-government, and began their life of freedom without being an integral part of an established world-wide pattern of trade and commerce, for much had been destroyed during the world conflict. Great imbalances in the social and economic structures of the countries existed, particularly in levels of skills and learning, and in the distribution of land ownership. Opportunities for generating employment were few, for the necessary organizational capacity, command of resources and capital, and properly established urban administrative institutions and systems did not exist. A well-established governmental administrative structure was not always part of the heritage of many of these countries when they began self-government.

National policies for economic development had to be totally reformulated, for accumulated wealth and capital resources were rarely to be found in the national treasury when they acquired their independence and assumed self-government. There was, of necessity, much preoccupation with establishing an administrative machinery to deal with these almost insurmountable problems of the nation, many of which were frighteningly dynamic in themselves, seemingly growing at too fast a rate for the economic resources of the country to be marshalled to deal with them effectively. It must be expected that there will be a lapse of time, perhaps much more than several decades, before sufficient resources, both in human skills or capital, can be accumulated, marshalled, and orientated by these governments to cope with the problem of stable economic development, as we understand the term today. Doubtless, new concepts of standards, levels, and values of urban living for these nations will need to be evolved to meet the problem within the prevailing circumstances.

The Urbanization Process — An Historical Example

For the most part in the cities of the developing nations today, the growth pattern is much the same, in principle, as that of all the great cities of the last millennium; the difference is that today the scale of the urban population involved is so immense, and their numbers are increasing at a rate seemingly beyond our comprehension.

Throughout the whole of the pre-industrialization era, i.e. pre-nineteenth century, there were factoral controls which restrained the rapid increase of urban or city population. Throughout Europe, the *birth rate* in the cities was estimated at approximately one-third only of that in the rural areas, while the *death rate* in the cities was three times as high as in the rural areas. There was a lessening of the death rate in the cities during the nineteenth century,[10] and in the case of cities such as London this can be understood. Up to the nineteenth century, the water supply for the city was mostly from wells and rivers into which cesspools and water from graveyards drained. For the greater part of the eighteenth century, London was dominated by a sense of the "waste of life" recorded in the Bills of Mortality, which were bills of burials and baptisms kept by the Company of Parish Clerks. Despite the excessive death rate, the population of London was estimated to have doubled from 674,000 in 1700 to 1,274,000 by 1820. This is attributed, to a certain degree, to the prosperity which the working class enjoyed over the early part of the period — a prosperity which attracted a high rate of in-migrants. The city was ravaged regularly by cholera, and life expectancy in London then was about 35 years; in Liverpool and Manchester, it was about 25 years. In those days, living in the city was always regarded as involving a much higher risk of epidemic

10. Kingsley Davis, "The Urbanization of the Human Population", *Scientific American,* September 1965, pp. 41–53.

and degenerative diseases (together with much discomfort) than living in the rural areas did.

Because of the advances made by the Government of Great Britain over the past century in evolving successful practices in urban development, and through the concept and effective implementation of a national urbanization programme, it is perhaps permissible to examine, in *very brief terms,* the way in which the urban slum-squatter problem of the past has been adjusted through the development of the local government administrative system. Perhaps it can be used as an indication of the process of city evolution through which all the great towns and cities of the developing world will need to progress, though at a greatly accelerated rate.

The city slums of eighteenth-century Britain appear to have grown up to meet the momentary demands of shelter for those who were crowding into the cities to obtain employment in the new industrial factories, though Dr. M. Dorothy George reveals that,[11] even as early as the latter part of the sixteenth century, "the speculative builder and investor in house property added their share to the chaotic development of London; they sprang into existence with the beginning of the rapid increase of population in the later sixteenth century". Usually, the in-migrants settled on the outer fringes of the cities, just outside the jurisdiction of the town oligarchies, few of whom had ever taken the trouble to meet the obligation of providing proper city services and administration even for their own town district. Shanty-towns, and jerry-built row-housing, with no controls or guidance, soon flourished, and rows and rows of depressed, cramped, poorly constructed houses, with little regard for proper community standards of space for decent living, soon grew rapidly to form the outskirts of all the industrial cities of the early nineteenth century. Quick profit for the builders was the only motivation, and it left in its wake a trail of social chaos over the following decades; as described by G. M. Trevelyan,[12] a "rampant individualism, inspired

11. M. Dorothy George, *London Life in the Eighteenth Century* ("Peregrine Books" [Harmondsworth, Middlesex: Penguin, 1966]), p. 87.
12. G. M. Trevelyan, *Illustrated English Social History* ("Pelican" [Harmondsworth, Middlesex: Penguin]), IV, 15.

by no idea beyond quick money returns, set up the cheap and nasty model of modern industrial life and its surroundings".

Under the Westminster Improvement Act of 1762 much had been done to improve urban living conditions, in at least one part of metropolitan London. Foot pavements were constructed, street lamps (which were alight all night) were installed, and a domestic water supply was provided. This was reticulated through wooden pipes, and connected to the houses by lead pipe connections, with water available three days a week. Fire plugs were installed in the streets, and new sewers were constructed (though these were defective enough by later standards). All this, together with the new and elegant houses in the superb squares of the West End, caused the comment in 1780 that "if all London were as well built, there would be nothing in the world to compare with it".[13]

But there was much of the urban problem for which the Improvement Acts were not responsible. The point of view of the Commissioners of the Westminster Improvement Act of the eighteenth century was that its sole purpose was urban improvement — that is, that it was to be used to remove nuisances of all kinds, which included dilapidated hovels, and their inhabitants. Civic pride was concerned with expensive rebuilding schemes, but not with humanity.[14] The Commissioners considered that the rookeries, the slum-squatter colonies in the many courts and alleys were outside their jurisdiction,

13. M. D. George. *op. cit.*, p. 76, quoting Archenholtz (*circa* 1780). See also p. 113 for quotation (dated 1826) by Francis Place, who had already described the rookeries as several of the most dirty, wretched, and miscreant neighbourhoods of the city: "In a few years from this time it will hardly be believed that an immense number of houses were built in narrow courts and close lanes, each house being at least three stories and many of them four stories above the ground floor. That in these courts and lanes the dirt and filth used to accumulate in heaps and was but seldom removed, that many of these tall houses had two or three and sometimes four rooms on a floor, and that from the garrets to the cellars a family lived or starved in each room. Circulation of air was out of the question, the putrid effluvia was always stagnant in these places, and had not London been in other respects a healthy place, the plague must still have continued among us."

14. *Ibid.*, p. 115.

and when any of these slum colonies were demolished it was for the sole purpose of opening up a new roadway. The fate of the people who inhabited the demolished rookeries was of no concern to the Commissioners; the families simply went to form new slum or squatter colonies in other parts of the city.

Nor was any provision made by the central or local authorities for housing the people dislodged from the demolished rookeries in the early nineteenth century. For the most part, as before, the demolition of the rookeries had only the effect of increasing the overcrowding in the parts which remained.

Appeals were made by some for a housing policy, in the interests of health and decency. But the ruling class of Britain at this time did not concede that town building, public health, sanitation, and the control of industrial and factory working conditions (along with the welfare of the workers) was any concern of government. In fact, housing policy was one of the last reforms to receive attention and only then after philanthropists began to take up the cause.

There were those, however, such as Robert Owen in 1817, who saw the need for giving some attention to the people of the towns; he saw in the new industrial system of the day an instrument for the standardized improvement of town design and layout throughout the entire country;[15] he saw it as a means of providing improved living and working conditions for the people as a whole. Owen propounded that environment makes character, and that our own environment is under our own human control. He believed that good work could be expected only from well-fed, well-clothed, and educated workers.

15. There are numerous references to the life and work of Robert Owen, including his own autobiography, *The Life of Robert Owen, Written by Himself* (London: E. Wilson, 1857); *Threading My Way: Twenty-Seven Years of Autobiography* (1874), written by his son, Robert Dale Owen; and a biography, written in retrospect by G. D. H. Cole in 1925, entitled *The Life of Robert Owen* (London: F. Cass, 1965), Owen wrote several volumes, following rather the concern of his age for the future improvement of society; amongst the most notable is *A New View of Society, or Essays on the Principle of the Formation of the Human Character,* published in 1813.

He demonstrated these principles in his administration of the mill and the factory at New Lanark, by improving the conditions of working and living for his employees, and showed how, in his opinion, the State should assume responsibility for, and enforce by law, the policy of proper standards of housing, public health and sanitation, hours of work, wages, welfare, and education for the great mass of industrial workers.

State control in the interests of the working class was not an idea which found much favour with the rulers of Britain during the Napoleonic conflict, but in 1835 a Municipal Reform Act was passed providing for the exercise by local government of a greater measure of control over urban development. In 1838, the Commissioners, under the new Poor Law of 1834, drew attention officially to bad housing and insanitary conditions as the cause of sickness and poverty.

It is of particular interest to note how the predominantly agrarian economy of the nation was changing; with the employment opportunities that were offering in the cities, the weight of population distribution had shifted to the industrialized urban centres, with the result that the Corn Laws of 1815, a legislative measure aimed at protecting farming land owners (at the expense of city consumers), were repealed in 1846 by the demand of the urban dwellers.

A Public Health Act was introduced in 1848, but it was permissive rather than compulsory, for it permitted municipalities to take deliberate action in matters of public health only if they were so inclined: many were not.

Even at late as 1864, cholera was prevalent in London. In that year, an illustration in *Punch*, by John Leech, entitled "A Court for King Cholera", depicts the overcrowded slums behind Oxford Street in London, and in the street the refuse piles, which were used as play-mounds by the children, and from which the scavengers gleaned some filthy morsel of food.[16] Similar scenes are with us today in many of the cities of the developing world.

It took more than twenty years before the Public Health Act was amended and actually made an instrumentality for public health. Fifty years were to elapse from the time of the Municipal Reform Act before an effective legislative measure

16. G. M. Trevelyan, *op. cit.*, Fig. 86.

for local government was evolved in Britain, i.e. the Local Government Act of 1888. This Act laid the foundation for the highly evolved modern local government system of today, embracing housing and town planning, the construction of new towns, and the administrative machinery to implement these policies and programmes, and ensuring an effective allocation of national funds from the country's annual budget in support of the national urban development programme.

By approximately 1900, the death rate in the cities of Britain had declined, life expectancy had been considerably extended, the birth rate was increasing, and the child mortality rate (still quite high in many of the developing countries today) had been reduced.

The urbanization process in Britain, begun on the basis of industrialization, was bringing about the evolution of a more comprehensive public administrative system to support the economic and human needs of the city. The importance of the role of the cities in national economic development was recognized, and recognized to the extent that the authority of local government was extended far beyond that envisaged by Adam Smith in his *Wealth of Nations*, in which he propounded, among other things, that government should provide only the "police and justice" within which the circumstances pertaining to the creation of wealth could flourish.

Whether and to what extent the government of the day in Britain was motivated by humanitarian motives, or by the necessity of preserving the nation's cities as the key to continued economic progress, or by the realization that the one is a vital component of the other, can always be a subject of lively debate.

What is important to note is that in Britain, as in so many of the high-density urbanized nations of Europe, the Government has, since the turn of the twentieth century, assumed an increasing responsibility for upgrading urban standards of living. It has done this by consciously making provision for efficient essential services, such as water supply and sanitation, urban housing, schools, communal services, etc., and by providing controls, through regulations, over building construction, and the use of urban land, and, most important of all, by providing an effective disciplined procedure and a budgetary allocation annually for the implementation of such provisions. In recent

years, the Government has extended the scope of its operations
to include the demonstration of the principle of re-establishing
urban society in a consciously planned settlement pattern of
new towns.

The evolution of such an effective local government administrative system for the city governments of the developing
world and the establishment of systems which can be effectively
implemented, the introduction of health and sanitation standards, building codes and regulations, road designs and specifi-
cations, tax collections, public services and security, with an
adequate number of properly trained personnel to make such
a programme effective — all this can hardly be accomplished
in a few years. Personnel must be trained, and the policies and
laws must be understood and accepted by the populace, most
of whom, having had little education, cannot comprehend the
complexities of urban life. There is also the vital component
of public leadership, and the test of the administrative system
by traditional practice. It usually requires several decades
before the populace have confidence in the system, and work
with the local authority to their mutual benefit. In this lies
the crux of the problem facing the prefects, mayors, and municipal authorities of many of the cities of the developing nations
today, in the face of the excessive movement into their jurisdictional areas of families from the poverty-stricken rural districts,
families who have no notions of urban living, or of the reciprocal
obligations between the resident population and the local
authorities — who, in fact, have little knowledge of the social
contract which exists between the two, but have only their own
intuition of their rights to self-preservation.[17]

A CHANGING URBAN SOCIETY MEANS A CHANGE IN THE SOCIAL
CONTRACT

In considering the growth of the British public administrative
system, embracing local government and housing, which
evolved as a result of the urbanization process set in motion
by eighteenth-century industrialization, it is important to note
also the philosophical basis of the system. It can be said that

[17.] See following footnote.

the system was a product of the social contract prevailing in that country, and in particular as it prevailed at that time.

There was a significant difference between the speculations on moral philosophy in Britain and France at the time, if we accept Thomas Hobbes[18] as the leader of political philosophical thinking in Britain, and Rousseau[19] as a clear exponent of logical thought on the subject amongst the French. Hobbes's version of the social contract was in support of the absolute power vested in the Sovereign of his day. Rousseau was searching for a framework of society based on a social bond in which men would be left as free as they were in a state of nature. This he regarded as the optimum of good society, and for this the people of the less developed nations today are intuitively searching.

It would appear that the majority of the developing countries which gained their independence in recent years from former Latin colonial powers are at the stage of self-awareness in which Britain, and particularly France, found themselves in the eighteenth century. There are many moral issues which have yet to be identified by the "body politic" of the developing nations, particularly as the body politic, on Rousseau's thinking, is a moral being, possessed of a General Will, which should tend always towards the preservation and welfare of the

18. Thomas Hobbes (1588–1679), one of the foremost English philosophers, made natural *right,* which was essentially the right to self-preservation, rather than the natural law, his fundamental concept. In his concept of the social contract, his "solution was to give a guarantee of the good behaviour of his fellows by creating a power sufficient to keep them in awe. This power will be created if each individual promises every other individual that he will carry out whatever commands some selected person — either one man or an assembly, but preferably one man — shall consider necessary for the peace and defense of all." The complete works of Hobbes were compiled by Sir William Molesworth, 1839–1845. Many other individual references are available, of which a valuable one is the recent *The Political Philosophy of Hobbes,* by Howard Warrender (London: Oxford University Press, 1957). See the *Encyclopaedia Britannica* (1961 edn.), II, 616, for additional references.

19. Jean Jacques Rousseau, *The Social Contract and Discourses,* translated with an Introduction by G. D. H. Cole (London: Dent), pp. V–XXX.

people as a whole, and should constitute, for all the members of the State, within their social contract, the rule of what is just or unjust.

The logic of Rousseau in arriving at his concept of the social contract can be applied to analyzing the trends of urbanization in the developing countries today, for many have newly written constitutions, the aim of which is to provide that every man shall be counted equal.

Many of the contemporaries of Rousseau regarded the "society of mankind" as possessing an innate "instinct of sociability", which gave rise to an inclusive "social obligation", binding all men together in terms of a common natural morality. To some extent, the way in which small groups of citizens exert their personal efforts in trying to help urban squatters, for instance, is a demonstration of this point, but the fact that it is only the efforts of a small number of individuals, and not invariable government policy, indicates that the principle is true only in part.

Rousseau rejected this hypothesis, and argued that society can be "accounted for, and justified, as a means of enabling men to advance to a higher level of achievement than could be arrived at in its absence". It was the necessary means to the development of the moral potentialities of man's original nature.

On this is based his concept of the social contract, which he represents as an agreement among men previously in a "state of nature" to constitute a "collective moral person", through which they endow themselves with a constitution or a code of laws designed to regulate both their mutual relations and their relations with other men.[20]

Some of the complexities of the urban squatter problem within the cities are to be found in the differences between the content of the social contract evolved by established urban society — a contract which has been modified and adjusted over the preceding generations to their own convenience — and that of the concept of communal co-existence which the squatter in-migrants are now evolving among themselves to suit their minimal needs.

20. *Ibid.*

The inhabitants of many of the urban squatter colonies of the developing world, who are a newly formed sub-group of urban society and not equipped or adjusted for assimilation into the present community structure, are now recognizing in themselves a "collective moral person". Because of their increasing numbers and voting strength, they are beginning to experiment with, test, and gradually cause to be adopted, through existing constitutional and legislative procedures, a change in the existing laws; these changes are drafted to suit their common convenience and the levels of living which are within their reach. However, with their increasing influence upon the legislature towards this end, there is a tendency to reduce all standards of organized living in the city to that of the lowest common denominator. In the case of city administrations which resist this reduction of urban standards, the gap between the squatters (who will soon constitute the majority of the population of these cities) and established urban society widens proportionally with the increase in the number of squatters and the absence of any organized programme for their social integration.

The constant succession of revolutions in Latin America, the Middle East, Africa, and Asia since the 1939–1945 war, and the racial riots in the United States in the 1960's, are a reminder of the maladjustment of the social contract which exists in such a large part of the world today.

Throughout recorded history, the living standards of the city have been the indicator of the level to which the organized society of that city has evolved. From the concentration and interchange of intellect within the confines of its cities, knowledge, wealth, and experiment over the centuries have provided mankind with scientific and technological advances sufficient to create and manipulate the physical, social, and economic environment in which men live, independently of that provided by nature.

It is the conscious collective and social activity of society, then, that over the centuries, from within the confines of the city, has made possible the control of economic conditions — a process quite unlike the procedure of natural selection which, without the collaboration of the individual, has governed the control and development of all organic life.

It is necessary to consider, if there is to be a conscious control over the squatter absorption of the cities which have this problem, on whom will devolve the duty of making the policy and decisions which will be responsible for the change in the urban administrative system, for the allocation of new priorities in the budgetary dispersion, for the design and maintenance of the city, and for ensuring that the city treasury will remain strong and the economy of the city continue to expand.

Traditionally throughout history, through the control and guidance of a "creative minority",[21] the city has grown up as a cohesive entity of various groups of socio-economically interdependent sub-societies. Within each of the sub-societies, the responsibility for the functioning of the city as a complex organic structure supported by technical mechanics has become sectoralized and delegated to sub-groups of the social structure through a hierarchy of disciplined procedures; today, the executive function is carried out mostly through the process of "city administration". The established inhabitants of most cities have assisted in formulating (and now submit to) the rules and laws prescribed for urban group living — such as those pertaining to payment of taxes, city hygiene and sanitation, collective use of space, police and security, to name but a few — and with continued experience over the decades, sometimes over the centuries, have participated in reshaping their urban environment to suit their collective convenience.

In the daily life of every city, the mechanics of water supply,

21.   As Professor Arnold Toynbee propounds (see footnote 8 above), if the leadership of the creative minority of a society fails to respond to this challenge, history has demonstrated that the society will inevitably decline. Unlike the people of agrarian communities, whose lives, economy, and dependence are closely identified with nature, the urban squatters are now dependent upon and have transferred their hopes for their future life to the city, a creation of society, or as Rousseau describes it, "of human artifice, not one of natural consequence". The squatters themselves, when they are in such numbers as to become the dominant group of common interest in a city, must exert a greater influence over the control of the city, and assume the leadership of the present "creative minority" of society — a role for which, it would appear, they are ill-prepared.

drainage, power supply, road designs and construction, and other such essentials permit the organic functioning of all the related components. All of these can be expressed as a dimension of space and land use, within which is contained the human element, occupying and utilizing that space.

As the political control of cities with an urban squatter problem passes from the presently established urban society, who for generations past have systematically built up and maintained the city as a thriving organism, into the hands of the emergent urban squatter society, who have little or no heritage of city-dwelling, and who at present have no training in or administrative knowledge of city-maintenance, it can be expected that essential services will diminish until they finally break down and collapse. In these circumstances, when the "creative minority", who over the years have moulded and shaped their environment, realize that they are no longer a force able to influence the improvement of society, they will depart for other cities where they can live at their own prescribed standard, leaving their former city in the hands of those who cannot properly manage it. Under such conditions the city will begin to fall into decay, and the lives of the occupants will become even more depressed, until their final extinction through a plague.

Breakdowns of water supply systems, power houses, drainage discharge systems, sewerage discharge systems, etc. are already a frequent occurrence in many of the cities of the developing nations today. The situation is deteriorating, not improving.

Eight years after the commencement of the United Nations Development Decade, the little evidence available indicates that a hopelessly insufficient amount of capital investment is being directed into dealing with the urban squatter problem of the cities, because amongst the present urban establishments there exists no moral philosophy adequate to adjust the social imbalances which are mounting every year.

In the post-war years, particularly in the less developed nations which have recently gained independence, city authorities and local governments have been accorded a great deal of local autonomy by the national governments. Provision has invariably been made in law (but rarely effectively applied) for annual grants of financial assistance from the national government, or national "body politic", to the local governments for urban improvement. Unfortunately, the "body politic" of most of the newly independent countries is having to accelerate the nation's social evolutionary process, but without the aid of a strong treasury, or the support of a high level of per capita productivity, or involvement in a prosperous and active trading system.

The role of the squatter society in the developing nations needs also to be examined within the concept of Rousseau's premise, that the life of citizens, i.e. occupants of a city, is based on the acceptance of an essentially artificial form of community inspired by the predominance of the General Will. When the urban squatter society finally dominates the city, their collective "will" becomes the General Will. The measure of the quality of that "will", their level of technical competence, and administrative discipline, their philosophical concept of the role of the city in regional economic development, and their decisions on what is just or unjust, will determine the extent to which the city can survive.

It is presumed that all urban squatters possess an intuitive sense of self-preservation, which, in their own minds, is a natural right (much after the philosophy of Hobbes).[22] That being accepted, one can concede that the squatter has an intuitive sense of social contract with his fellow squatters, and is also willing to concede the existing written or constitutional contract — until a stage is reached where the pressure for self-survival is felt. At this point, he would revert to his own intuitive sense of justice, and, if necessary for his own survival, arrange for a new written social contract.

THE SHIFTING BALANCE OF RURAL TO URBAN POPULATION

In the towns and cities of eighteenth-century Europe, the growing poverty, so noticeable in the midst of such apparent plenty and elegance, gave rise to much social philosophical speculation. Thomas Malthus[23] hypothesized that it is an

22. See footnote 18 above.
23. Thomas Robert Malthus, *First Essay on Population, 1798* (A reprint in facsimile of *An Essay on the Principle of Population As It Affects the Future Improvement of Society* [1798]; London: Macmillan, 1966), pp. 10–14.

incontestable truth that population, if unchecked by war, famine, or pestilence or any other means, will increase at a geometric rate, and that this increase is a fundamental natural force, whilst the means of subsistence for the population can increase only at an arithmetic rate.

Because of its increase in numbers, and the need for daily subsistence, mankind has spread itself across the face of the earth, and is multiplying most noticeably in geographic regions which possess the most tolerable physical environment, where families can survive most easily. Though man has been breeding at a high rate in these tropical and temperate zones, the capacity of the land to support the increasing numbers, within the prevailing land tenure systems, and to sustain them at tolerable levels of living, has diminished, with the result that many have turned to what appears to them to represent the image and hope of prosperity, the "city".

Annual population increase in most cities of the developing world is averaging nearly 6 per cent, whilst the annual increase in the number of squatters (who constitute a part of the total) varies, but in many cases is as high as 12 per cent, and sometimes 15 per cent.

This was demonstrated in studies carried out in the Philippines, in India, and in Latin American countries. Recent studies by the Government of Brazil indicate that the population growth per annum of the various towns and cities varies from 4 per cent to 10 per cent, with an average of more than 5 per cent for all cities, while the rural population is increasing at only 0.8 per cent per annum. Because of the known high birth rate in the rural areas, this figure indicates an excessive rural-to-urban migration. By 1964, the rural and urban populations of the nation were equal, i.e. 40 million in each; but by 1976 the urban population is expected to increase to 66.6 million, whilst the rural population is expected to number no more than 43.5 million persons.[24] On present trends, it is estimated that the urban squatter population in 1976 for this

---

24. *Plano Decenal de Desenvolvimento Econômico e Social,* Tomo VI, *Desenvolvimento Social,* No. 5, *Habitação,* Ministry of Planning, Government of Brazil, 1966.

country alone will be 25 million[25] if no concerted programme is undertaken by the government to relieve the squatter or *favela* programme.

The towns and cities of the developing world (which account for nearly 100 of the 126 member-nations of the United Nations), estimated to be reaching a population in 1980 of between 1,700 million and 1,850 million, and probably 5,000 million[26] by the turn of the century, are already in the throes of a social transformation. Within the perimeters of the cities, a large new form of urban society is emerging and growing at an incredibly fast rate — the landless society of the urban squatters. Worse than being denied the opportunity of holding title to land, or the means of attaining a level of living in which their families can live in a reasonable standard of shelter, with sufficient food to sustain good health, is the fact that the urban squatters are *not* being absorbed into or integrated within the many established urban societies, despite the several government programmes. They are not finding a place in the social and economic structure of the community at a rate even partially commensurate with their rate of increase in the cities.

Without a massive urban squatter integration or relocation programme, it is expected that within twenty years the number of squatters will be far in excess of the population figures for the established city dwellers. Such a programme must be undertaken by this established urban society, backed by the full resources of the various national governments. It must upgrade the capabilities of these great multitudes of squatters, and integrate them, and orientate them in the mechanics of city administration, including the essential maintenance of

25.   The Government of Brazil, having a quantitative assessment of the problem, has already, by law, directed that the savings and investment of the people for retirement and pension benefits shall be invested in housing, predominantly low-cost housing. The capital is invested through the housing programme of the National Housing Bank, which, up to the end of 1967, under the Presidency of Dr. Mario Trindade, was able to finance the construction of nearly 200,000 dwellings, and, over the period 1969–1970, plans to erect 715,000 dwellings throughout the country in a planned urbanization programme.

26.   See Tables B and C in chapter 1.

capital formation and productivity. If this is not done, it would appear to be an historical inevitability that the squatters will assume the role of "body politic", i.e. will assume political control of the cities, without knowing how to retain essential discipline, and without the expertise necessary to maintain the complex mechanics involved in the administration of a city.

New systems of administrative practice, new values and priorities for city budgetary allocations, new forms of tax collections and additional obligations will have to be accepted by the state and city authorities to adjust existing social and economic imbalances. An energetic programme, such as that outlined above, has become an urgent necessity.

Even the more sophisticated and advanced nations, such as the United States, have come to the realization that a "new philosophy for cities" is necessary. As Professor Charles Abrams propounds:[27] "It is late, but not too late to alter the stream of events. But it will require a change in the nation's philosophy." Professor Abrams defines six aspects of the new philosophy, which the nation needs to acknowledge, and which can be summarized as follows:

(a) that there are values worth preserving in the cities in contrast with the suburbs; they constitute a diversity of environments in which to live, work, and raise one's family. They are still the vital influence in national life and the market places of trade, experimentation, and ideas.

(b) that the central city and suburbs are an entity, interdependent for job opportunities, services, recreation, escape, variety, and progress. The suburb is as unique to America as the decline of its cities; the suburb may have to cope with the racial problems which the cities are facing. As the suburb spreads out further onto the millions of acres which it will consume, the limits of travel may be reached and the suburbias may decline just as the older cities have declined.

(c) that there is the necessity to redefine city, state, and federal functions in fulfilling the needs and provisions of general welfare.

27. The material quoted has been summarized from Charles Abrams, *The City Is the Frontier* (New York: Harper and Row, 1967), pp. 360–65.

(d) that the government's philosophy should be to assure the citizens the right to live where they choose. As the historic refuge, the city's doors must be open to all. Unless the national government intervenes with subsidies and enforcement of laws to make it possible for the poor to live where they choose and in homes that are decent, "the right to move is a shell". Neither city nor any government entity, old or new, can function as the enclave of a single class or race.

(e) that low-income families are entitled to the opportunity to own homes and to own them without fear of losing them when unemployment, illness, or death supervenes.

(f) that poverty is a national concern. Because poverty now exists mostly in the cities, the cities as well as poverty must be part of a national responsibility ... It means that the national government must take on many obligations that the old city can no longer bear, and which the state is no longer posed to do. This entails a re-examination of the nation's tax system, its re-adaptation to the needs of urban society, and the re-deployment of revenues to meet the needs and responsibilities of people wherever they live.

The urban squatters are inherently searching for an improvement in their personal and family circumstances; the exact level of their collective aspiration for improvement is still a subject requiring particular enquiry. There already exists a gradation of the living standards of the entire squatter hierarchy, from the excessively primitive squalor in which some live, to the large, well-constructed houses of those at the other end of the scale; but, for several reasons, very few hold positions of employment beyond that of assistant artisan.

The search for a comprehensive urban planning process and a system of city administration which is an acceptable compromise between the rights of the existing established urban citizens and those of the increasing numbers of squatter families is the challenge which faces urban planners and those responsible for urban administration and development in the less developed nations of today.

There exists, in many of the newly independent nations, a very wide range of ethnic groups, each at various levels on the scale of social evolution. Socially, the problem is far more complex than that which European cities had to face in the eighteenth century. In the Philippines, for example, the ethnic groups range from the negroid Igorots, and the head-hunting Ilongots in the mountainous regions in the north, to the Moros from Mindanao in the south, and the sophisticated descendants of the landowning Spanish families of the cities; in Brazil, from the Indians in the Amazonas Region to the technologically advanced "elite" families of Portuguese descent in the cities of the south. Much the same can be said of many of the developing nations.

It is late, but not too late, as Professor Abrams says, to alter the stream of events. Over the past millennium, education has led society to learning, and thence to knowledge, and this in turn has led to collective agreement and action for mutual security, increased production, and the improvement of society. Standards of living permitting the fuller development of the family have been established and adjusted, and the scientific method applied to manipulate all the resources at the disposal of society for raising the existing standards of living.

Much the same applies to the present urban squatter society. Given special attention through a carefully contrived educational programme, one which is adjusted to the various comprehension levels of the in-flowing migrants, the adults can be orientated, at least mentally, to the requirements of urban living. They can be equipped with a skill or a trade, whereby they may become persons with a capacity for output and productivity; they can then gravitate into the established low-income society of the town, thus taking the first step in the social evolutionary process for their families. The first generation of these squatter families, having been given education as children, could integrate with existing urban society much more easily and naturally. With people who are literate, and able to take their place in the structure of society, it is possible for the planners to devise new concepts for the collective use of space within a proper socio-economic frame of reference.

THE EVOLUTION OF A SCIENTIFIC METHOD FOR THE DIAGNOSIS AND CONTROL OF URBANIZATION

In the eighteenth century, the pressure of population was being felt in both cities and countryside throughout Europe, but the actual numbers of in-migrants to cities such as London were not known until the census of 1811, which followed the census of 1801. Thomas Malthus had been collating and analyzing all the demographic and economic data available at the time, and in 1803 drew the conclusion (which was an elaboration of his *Essay on the Principle of Population As It Affects the Future Improvement of Society* [1798]) that the population, when unchecked, increases in a "geometric ratio", whilst subsistence increases only at an "arithmetic ratio".

He asserted that the realization of a happy, socially balanced, and integrated society will always be hindered by the miseries consequent upon the tendency of the population to increase faster than the means of providing subsistence, and that the population increase will be governed by the limits of the production and means of distribution of the subsistence, and such other positive checks as war, famine, and pestilence. His doctrine was one of "moral restraint", and history has vindiated his thesis. The governments of the world, working on an international basis, have combined their efforts on such projects as the United Nations World Food Programme, the Freedom from Hunger Campaign, and many others, to redistribute the available surplus of food; but there has been a significant absence of "moral restraint" on the part of the population of the world. The numbers continue to surge upwards, and a high percentage of these people are receiving nutrient intakes far below recommended averages; the problem is compounded by the annual recurrences of drought and flood which cause famine in many parts of the world.

The Rev. Thomas Malthus

During the latter part of the eighteenth century, there was much speculation on the "future improvement of society", and the Reverend Thomas Malthus, whose father was an executor of the estate of Rousseau, elucidated his thoughts on the matter in 1798, and published his *Essay on the Principle of Population, As It Affects the Future Improvement of Society*. He was ill-prepared for the controversy which followed, because, as he realized even as he wrote his essay, there was so little quantitative evidence to support his hypothesis. His basic thesis has been vindicated,

a century and a half later, in the social philosophical problem
of the developing world.

There were those who propounded that the best argument in
support of the ultimate perfectibility of man and society could
be drawn from a contemplation of the great progress that had
already been attained at that time, known as the "Age of
Elegance"; society having originated from the savage state,
it was difficult to say where the progress would stop.

Malthus argued that the power of population increase was
infinitely greater than the power of the earth to produce
subsistence for man. The world of the twentieth century has
reached a most remarkable level of scientific achievement.
Agricultural science can theoretically extract optimum subsistence from the soil and the sea; why, then, in the latter part
of the twentieth century, is half the world suffering from malnutrition and why do hundreds of thousands of children die
annually from starvation?

As the nations of Europe evaluated their progress in the late
eighteenth century, there seemed every reason to suppose that
man would henceforth continue with accelerated velocity
towards illimitable, and hitherto unconceived improvement;
Malthus argued that society would be condemned to perpetual
oscillation between happiness and misery, and after every
effort remain still at an immeasurable distance from the wished-
for goal. In retrospect, the societies of the northern and southern
latitudes have progressed considerably, while most societies of
the sub-tropical to tropical zones are still an immeasurable
distance from such goals.

In analyzing the national cash flow, using what information
was available, he came to the conclusion that the Poor Laws
of England, relying on the charity of the Parish, were working
against the improvement of society. He came to the conclusion
that by giving a poor man only money others of the same class
are depressed. The way to benefit a poor man without depress-
ing others in his same class would be either to retrench the
quantity of food consumed in a rich man's house and give that
to the poor, or to "turn up" an uncultivated piece of land and
give him the produce, whereupon both would be benefited,
the rich and the poor, as would be all members of society.
Giving the poor man money without increasing the common

stock of food only raises the price of food to the detriment of all.

Malthus contended that the Poor Laws acted to diminish both the power and the will to save among the common people, and thus weakened the strongest incentives to sobriety and industry amongst the people. The parish environment provided little or no incentive for the poor to use their time profitably or productively.

Dr. Adam Smith had already prescribed his concept of the wealth of the nation, which he measured as the annual produce of the land, and the labour.

In his day, the rural-urban migrations were noticeable, and the poor in the towns and cities were increasing obviously in number, much the same as the poor urban squatters-in the towns and cities of the developing nations today. Malthus could see no avenue of employment for them except as casual labourers, and it was in this that he pointed out the fallacy of the premise of Adam Smith, in that, as he explains:

> If a nation were to add what it saved from its yearly revenue only to the manufacturing capital of the country, and *not* to the investment capital employed on the land, it is evident that it will grow richer according to the above definition, without the power of supporting a great number of labourers, and therefore, without an increase in the real funds for the maintenance of labour.

Mechanization of the land can continue the high productivity of foodstuff from the land with less labour, but there is a limit to the extent to which the manufacturing industries can absorb unskilled labour, particularly 150 years later, when, with modern advances in technology, manufacturing industries are turning towards automation, using less labour wherever possible.

Malthus challenged that Dr. Adam Smith's enquiry into the nature and cause of the wealth of nations omits the cause and the happiness and comfort of the lower orders of society, which, as he recognized in his day, are the most numerous class in every society.

The medium through which the cities of the developing nations today and tomorrow will be able to generate wealth at a geometric rate to match the growth of population, rather as "industrialism" served the purpose in the nineteenth century in the confines of European towns and cities, has yet to be established.

Whereas Rousseau's social and political philosophy originated from observations on the social environment of the day
rather than from scientific criteria, Malthus was amongst the
first to realize the importance of a national quantitative system
for measuring the trends and consequences of population
growth; there was still no system, however, on which the real
behaviour and trends of the various sectors of society in both
city and country could be defined or understood quantitatively,
in terms of political economy.

Poverty in itself was not thought of as a crime which could
be punished, or against which the authorities could exercise
a strategy, as in a campaign; it was something deserving of
charity. The *consequences* of poverty — petty theft, or crime —
were summarily dealt with by the gallows, or the prisons, or
by transportation to the colonies. Except for the study on
demography by Malthus, there was no scientific method or
system by which the *trend* of growing urban poverty or the
consequences of growing social and economic urban imbalances
could be studied and systematically analyzed in such a way
that both the government and the people could decide how
best to deal with the problem and possibly adjust the social
contract to meet the needs of society as a whole; the problem
could not be quantified.

Frédéric Pierre Guillaume Le Play

The first to begin to use a scientific method for identifying the
social and economic factors on which the behaviour and trends
of the people of a city depend, and the relationship between
family and town, was Frédéric Pierre Guillaume Le Play, a
French mining engineer who, after witnessing the appalling
living conditions in the mining areas and industrial towns
throughout Europe during the early nineteenth century, and
after extensive travels throughout Eurasia, turned his attention
to the apparent difficulties impeding the improvement of
society. He lamented the fact that, despite his previous endeavours in the field of social reform, whilst he was a member of
the Council of State, the Government would not accept a
methodology for evaluating the various social constitutions
of Europe and using the best models as a guide to future policy.

He realized that, in the formation of new systems of government, more reliable guides were needed than "the passions of opponents or the egotism of the self-satisfied".[28]

His enquiry emanated from the suffering in Europe in the early nineteenth century. He could see two principal causes: one, the "l'erreur fondamentale" of corruption in England, Germany, and France, as identified by Rousseau (along with the premise that man is born innocent, it being only the environment of society that is corrupting); and the other, the exaggerated conglomeration of peoples crowded together over the coal basins of Europe, all serving the new manufacturing industries which were made possible by the steam engine. The excessive wealth which was created by this industrial revolution caused many of the leaders of the day to ignore the human element and values of life of the great mass of human beings engaged in contributing significantly to the creation of this wealth.[29]

He began firstly to define the important relationship between family types and the rest of society in both rural and urban areas. He analyzed and adjusted some of the concepts of Rousseau's Social Contract, within the environment of the Industrial Revolution, as he saw it at the time, and applied his theories to the concept of a balanced rural-urban inter-dependent society. Le Play worked to have Napoleon III and his Court re-create and preserve the "French family system", which kept the main branch of the family intact on an undivided homestead, whilst the remainder of the family were intended to enter government, government service, industry, civic life, and any other influential or productive pursuit in the city.

He set about evolving a scientific method for quantifying the family-city relationship; he began his studies always from the datum point of the family budget for the various levels of society. His studies then extended to cover the relation between the workers and industry, and then the relationship between

28.   Frédéric P. G. Le Play, *The Organization of Labour in Accordance with Custom and Law*, trans. Herbertson, "Difficulties and Their Solution", chapter VI, p. 297.

29.   F. P. G. Le Play, *La Constitution essentielle de l'humanité*, chapter VI, p. 205.

industry and the total population. After identifying the various values of income, its sources, expenses, and their uses, Le Play then extended his work to cover the moral attitudes of, and the relationship between worker, employer, government, and society, from which was derived his most notable work, *La Constitution essentielle de l'humanite.*

He drew some stimulus from Xenophon's *Memoirs of Socrates* and propounded that any nation which may be placed under similar circumstances (such as those pertaining to Athens), in order to prevent complete decline, has only to make use of two means:

(i) follow the best usage existing in other countries;
(ii) add to the best usage of former prosperous times others which are in harmony with the necessities of the present.

He analyzed the difficulties which were apparently obstructing the improvement of society, and therefore causing misery and suffering amongst so many people, particularly the labouring class in the mining and industrial centres of France and Germany in his time. He proposed a careful study, and imitation, of the best models which were known at the time throughout Europe, under the following subject headings:

1. The natural conditions which dispose people to entertain respect for God, and maintain public tranquillity
2. The religious institutions in which respect for God has been preserved
3. Civil institutions which best contribute to the preservation of public peace
4. Models of private family life, the place of labour, the Parish, and the Corporation
5. Models of Local Government in the Rural Department and City Commune
6. Models of Central Government, in the Province, and in the State.

During the latter part of the nineteenth century, all academic schools were inclined towards the idea of continuous evolutionary progress. Le Play evolved a contrary theory, that of cyclical changes in society with increases or decreases of family morale. His predictions of the future weakness of the society of Europe won him little popularity at the time.

Le Play, however, laid the basis for quantitatively examining the relation between rural and urban society, and for setting out the social and economic hierarchy of urban society. This covered only part of the urban scene, for there is also an essential physical and biological dimension in all urban growth and expansion, which had not been defined previously, and therefore could not be related in the same quantitative dimension of measurement as that of the social and economic factors.

Sir Patrick Geddes

During part of his education in Paris, in 1879, Patrick Geddes, formerly a student of Professor Thomas Huxley at the Royal School of Mines, London, and later Professor of Botany at Dundee University, came in direct contact with the theories of Le Play. Geddes saw in the city an essential biological structure. By extending the work and principles of Le Play, and by utilizing the biological laws governing the behaviour and response patterns of the individual, he evolved an acceptable scientific method for diagnosing a town or city in its regional environment. This method has since been used as the basis for modern-day civic and regional planning. It involves basically a process of diagnosis, ·analysis, and synthesis of all the factors related to urban growth and development. He was able to demonstrate that the development of human communities was essentially based on a biological process; therefore, the remedy for urban sickness would depend upon an accurate diagnosis of the complex interrelation between people, their environment, and their activities. He extended the hypothesis of Le Play, which he considered to be the "passive" side of an essential equation, "place, folk, work", to include achievement, synergy (synthesis of energy), polity, which was the "active" side of the equation of the formulae ("environment, function, and organization").[30]

His work resolves into a comprehensive concept the social philosophy of Rousseau, the statistical method and demographic system of Malthus, the principles of community environmental

[30]. Sir Patrick Gedbes, *Cities in Evolution* (London: Williams and Norgate), pp. 200–205.

adjustment and control of Robert Owen, the quantitative
system for measuring and synthesizing rural-urban interdependence, the relation of the family budget to national economic
structure, as prescribed by Le Play, and the dynamic biological
processes of city life, behaviour, and growth, as a multiple
expression of the individual, as identified by his own scholar-
ship.[31]

Although the present trend of increasing urban squatting
in the modern-day cities of the developing world gives every
cause for deep concern, the members of government, the public
administrators, and the professional consultants and advisers
to all the governments afflicted with the problem have at their
disposal the benefit of a scientific method which has been
evolved over the experience of 150 years in Europe. From this
system can be drawn a method for the diagnostic survey,
analysis, synthesis, and projection of the trends of the various
sectors of urban growth, and from it remedial legislative and
economic measures can be introduced to correct the present
widening human, economic, and social imbalances existing in
so many of these towns and cities in the world today.

[31.] There are many publications which graphically illustrate the
application of the diagnostic method of Patrick Geddes to urban
planning, but a valuable technical reference and well-illustrated
model of procedure, applicable to the developing world, is
*Kaduna, 1917–1967–2017: A Survey and Plan of Kaduna and Its
Capital Territory, Nigeria*, by Max Lock and Partners (London:
Faber and Faber, 1966).

CHAPTER FIVE

Planning Towards a Rural-Urban Balance of Population

Urbanizing the Pioneer Fringes of the Developing Nations

The preceding sections have endeavoured to demonstrate that throughout the many developing nations of the world today, whether in Latin America, Asia, or Africa, there exists an increasingly large percentage of the population which does not benefit from the expansion of the country's economy. The annual increase of the gross national product for the developing countries, though fluctuating considerably for several countries, year by year, on average, is about 4–5 per cent; yet the number of families suffering from multiple deficiencies such as lack of employment, lack of education, lack of technical skills, lack of adequate shelter or housing, inadequate levels of environmental sanitation, and low nutritional intake, is increasing in most of the developing countries.

If we must concede the historical inevitability of a continuous shift from rural to urban living, then it can be acknowledged that there is no actual shortage of land for urban purposes; the problem lies in a deficiency of adequately equipped urban centres capable of absorbing this continuing shift in population into the productive employment structure of the towns. A corollary to this is a deficiency in the supporting capacity of the land in relation to the geographical distribution of the existing network or pattern of those towns or cities.

Before the Industrial Revolution in Europe in the eighteenth century, a clear pattern existed of the network of villages and towns based on agrarian pursuits, in their hierarchy of functions (marketing, collegiate, administration, port, craft industry, etc.), and in their various sizes in relation to their ascending scale of dimension;[1] each town had its own measurable sphere of influence, with an interdependence with other towns for reciprocal marketing, and social and other cultural entertainment, in a hierarchy of size, function, and travelling distance between centres.

With the establishment of growing industrial enterprises in some cities, and, in some cases in Europe, the emergence of new cities based on the location of industrial raw materials, the pattern of settlement, founded originally on an agrarian economy, suffered a considerable change or distortion. Among many industrial processes there is a continuity of process, which for the sake of efficiency and higher output capacity results in the extension of the original industry into a whole series of industrial establishments, constructed in close proximity one to the other. These in turn attract more workers, who, in turn, must be supported with consumer commodities, finance, and credit offices, recreational facilities, social services, and housing; and so the urbanization process continues to expand at an accelerated rate, related to the industrial processes.

The agrarian economy has ceased to be adequate to satisfy the need for capital formation in most developing countries, and yet the technological level of the majority of the people is still agrarian-orientated. *Urban industrialization* in the majority of cities in the developing world is not able to expand and create employment opportunities or stimulate capital formation at anything like the same rate as unskilled labour is flooding into the cities. It is possible, however, through a scientific assessment of the population-supporting capacity of the land, and through a guided urbanization programme, to rationalize the rural-

---

1. Geographer Christaller was able to demonstrate the hierarchy and pattern of settlement which was the result of an agrarian economy from the evidence of settlement patterns in Germany and East England. See W. Christaller, *Central Places in Southern Germany*, trans. C. W. Baskin (Englewood Cliffs, N.J.: Prentice-Hall, 1966), pp. 28–30.

urban settlement pattern throughout the land to provide a more equitable distribution in levels of living. There exist in most of the developing countries large tracts of territory with good fertile soil and an abundance of natural products, which, if properly settled and developed, could absorb a large number of selected families in a network of new villages and new towns — not with the same expensive urban "equipment and furniture" as the big cities have, but at levels of urban living which would satisfy the needs of many families. To name but a few such regions — in Indonesia, there are large unsettled areas in Borneo; in the Philippines, there is good land available in Mindanao; in Central Africa, there are the large river basins and systems, such as the Niger, Volta, and Congo river systems; and in Brazil there is the Amazon River basin.

In a study of personal preferences carried out in the Philippines among the urban squatters, approximately 50 per cent had a preference for returning to agrarian pursuits, *provided* that their families had convenient access to normal urban or communal facilities, health services, schools, marketing, etc.[2]

Should such an attitude prevail among the majority of urban squatters throughout the developing world today (and this has yet to be determined), then, coupled with the extension of the existing pattern of settlement within the pioneer fringes of the country, it may well constitute a basis for diverting the migration trend away from the larger towns and cities towards these new agro-industrial centres. This would give the city authorities an opportunity to proceed systematically with the modernization of their cities without the hindrance and burden imposed on them by having their populations continually increased by a vast number of socially and economically misplaced persons.

Most of the developing nations have their own "pioneer fringes" throughout which their governments could undertake a planned redistribution of population, supported by incentives and a guided programme of rural urbanization. The location of the new agricultural villages should be directly related with the settlement supporting capacity of the land.

2. M. Juppenlatz, *Housing the People in the Philippines* (United Nations, Office of Technical Co-operation, T.A.O./PHIL/14, 10 July 1968).

Malaya

Above—"Core house" provided for relocation of squatters into new agrarian-type villages. (Photograph taken 1962.)
Below—Extension of the "core house" by self-help to accommodate larger family. (Photograph taken 1962.)

Such a programme requires, however, a high degree of organizational and administrative skill on the part of the government. It necessitates the introduction of multidisciplinary procedures, and the application of scientific and technological methods in the advanced planning and in the implementation stages, all of which requires a deliberate allocation of funds from the national budget and the raising of capital from private sources. There must exist in the government concerned a recognition that the urbanization process is, in itself, of vital economic consequence to the development of the nation, demanding a high priority in national investment and development plans, and that it also represents a culmination of a large segment of most of the interdependent factors which are classified as necessary for national development.[3]

It is, however, conceded that in many of the developing countries there is an inadequate number of persons in government service who possess the experience or training necessary for the actual implementation of such rural planning and development projects. Many of the governments have not yet been able to establish effective regional development authorities, embracing geographical regions beyond the political boundaries of the provinces.

If a government is not adequately equipped to institute such resettlement and redevelopment projects, and yet their implementation becomes a matter of urgency for national survival, then it is possible to revert to historical experience and examine the feasibility of initiating such a programme of development through specially created joint stock development

3. An example of such a programme was given in the *Jornal do Brazil*, 8 May 1968, when notice was given of the intention of the Government of Brazil to commence a Pilot Project for the Industrialization and Settlement of the Amazon River basin. A special Ministerial Committee was created under the chairmanship of the Minister of Interior to initiate and supervise the project. Many agencies of the Government are involved in supporting the project, including Army engineering battalions, Air Force transport aircraft, naval contingents, and other units of the military forces. The project will be conducted within the administrative framework of the existing regional development authority, the Superintendency for the Development of the Amazon (SUDAM).

companies, or corporations, much after the fashion of the East India Company founded in 1602. The government could retain a controlling interest in such a company, but the whole project would be based on the development of trade and marketing, evolved from the natural products and capability of the land. Efficiency of production, land utilization, human resources, industry, processing and marketing — these must then be the criteria for the performance of the company. The development rights and title of the agreed territory must, of necessity, be transferred to the company. The intention and purpose of such companies is to accelerate the process of capital formation, thus raising the standard of living, and also to extend trading and commercial activities over a wider geographical area of the country. It is essential that the actual physical pattern of regional settlement, the minimum levels of living, and the interrelation of the sizes of towns in the regional setting should conform to a national urbanization programme, and, in that sense, it is important that the government retain a controlling interest in the company.

There should already be in existence a government policy on the development of all cities, on the nodes or centres of polarity upon which the hierarchy of settlement of the district is dependent, on the size to which a city can develop within a specific period of time, and therefore on the associated capacity and variety of function expected of that town, on the standards and levels of living, the economic productivity, and the continued rate of investment; all these matters need to be outlined, in policy, at least.[4] This is perhaps easier to attain in nations which have a centrally planned economy than it is in those nations where the authority of the national government has been extensively dispersed to local authorities. The creation of national development companies, which should be given jurisdiction over the region and charged with the responsibility for its comprehensive development (except in the case of any towns in the region which already possess local autonomy, when special agreements would need to be made), can be the means of achieving a substantial expansion of the economy

---

4. See Appendix I for outline of procedure for compiling data on which an urbanization policy can be formulated.

through this process of establishment, by the companies for and on behalf of the government, of new patterns of settlement.

In managing such projects through a development company, consideration should be given to the creation of subsidiary companies, each responsible for one of the following fields — industrial activities and processes, agricultural engineering, forest working, building construction, transport and communication, trading and marketing, etc. Such companies could be financed initially by government purchase of 51 per cent of preferential shares, with the balance of required capital being obtained from the sale of shares to the private sector, and to persons with vested interests in the region. The operation of such companies needs to be within the regional development policy of the government, but after a number of years, as the strategic industrial enterprises are established, and the settlement pattern with trade, communication, and the infrastructures established, the government could gradually transfer ownership of the stock to the people and to enterprises in the region.

In the case of most attempts at river-basin development, previous individual efforts to penetrate and settle the tropical forests have not been successful because of the rate at which the forest re-establishes itself; distances were too great for marketing, and for normal social intercourse, and the villages too small for the attainment of a quantity of production substantial enough to allow the families to escape from a subsistence economy.

As is the case at present with most of the great river basins in the tropical zones, where so little organized settlement has been established, the trade and commerce, and the economic expansion and planned settlement pattern could be based on the existing natural products, and employment created within the following fields:

   I. The lumber industry
      a) construction lumber
      b) special woods for joinery and furniture
      c) paper-pulp making
  II. Tropical fruits and vegetables — processed for export
 III. Vegetable oils

IV. Agricultural products — processed for local and external
    consumption
 V. Fish processing and protein products
VI. Rationalization of rubber plantations
VII. Extractive industries, such as mining and quarrying, etc.

   In this technological age, it is now highly feasible to install
industrial processes on ships and river craft, and float the
"industry" to its location. This is already a well-established
process in the fishing industry; the same process can be extended
to include food-processing plants, paper-pulp mills,[5] and others.
This concept facilitates the efficient erection of the industrial
plant under factory conditions in a highly advanced technological condition, and immediate operation when delivered to the
site. In this way the costly erection process of the industry in
isolated tropical forest areas is avoided, and the industrial
process has a mobility in itself and can be moved from place
to place in the region to service several new settlements.
   It can be the means of stimulating productivity and capital
formation during the early and usually critical years of a new
settlement programme in isolated areas.
   Settlement throughout a region of similar land and soil
characteristics usually gravitates naturally into a hierarchy or
relationship according to size, distance, and accessibility on
the basis of time taken to travel between the centres.[6] It is
often possible to accelerate the natural trend of settlement-
spread by selecting existing urban nuclei, and equipping and
establishing them as a base of operations from which to
penetrate the forests. What is particularly important in such
a programme is the logistical support necessary to coincide
with the family settlement programme, and for this the resources
of the Armed Forces could be used profitably for national development.
   The initial settlement pattern for such projects can be based
on "development units", or agricultural villages, each settled

   5. A floating paper-pulp mill for use in tropical forest river basins
      has been designed, and widely publicized, by A. B. Civil-
      engineering, and Eriksbergs Mekaniska Verkstad, Gothenburg,
      Sweden.
   6. Established by geographer, *Christaller*. See footnote 1 of this
      chapter.

initially with a population of 400 trained and selected families, or approximately 2,000 persons (rather similar to the original concept of Robert Owen [see p. 215]), each connected by overland road with the existing urban nuclei, or towns.

Usually, in tropical forest river systems, the towns are situated only on the river banks and are accessible (and can be serviced) by fast river craft. As the roadways penetrate the jungle from the selected town or development node which can provide the logistical support for the operation, the timbers cut can be selected and hauled back to a floating industrial plant for processing. The forest can be systematically cleared for agricultural settlement, and the timber used both for development, and for sale to create wealth. The size of the various villages can be planned to vary according to the supporting capacity of the land, the distances between the villages, and accessibility as regards supply of the various personal and communal needs.

It could be considered a valid strategy to endeavour to connect the existing urban nuclei on two separate rivers on a "primary line" of road construction, starting the construction from two existing urban centres at the same time, and penetrating the forest to meet at a suitable position. Here a major supply depot and urban community could be established, and from here the transverse penetration of the forest, i.e., parallel with and between the rivers, for the expansion of land settlement and forest utilization, and an acceleration of the "planned settlement", could be commenced.

A training programme to instruct the selected families in jungle survival, environmental and community sanitation, home economy and home craft, agricultural co-operatives and management, organization of credit unions, community organization and management, etc., is an essential prerequisite for such settlement programmes, if the villages are to prosper economically.

One way of systematically settling and extending the agricultural villages would be to build up the settlement programme on a "basic unit" or work force, each basic unit comprising forty families, all volunteers, and all with an aptitude for pioneering agricultural and agrarian pursuits or related community service. The proportion of agricultural field workers to village artisans, management officials, etc., would vary, but their proportion, approximately, would be two to one.

The basic units, related directly to each other in the *physical land use plan,* could be added to in a time sequence, one unit being added every two or three months; this would allow the gradual social integration of the various groups until the population reached some 2,000 persons, a number which in itself would economically justify such elementary community facilities as a primary school, health clinic, marketing centre, administration centre, home industry and craft centre, etc., and which would generate a sufficient variety of activity to sustain a high level of morale. Maintaining a high level of morale in isolated communities should be the responsibility of the parent company, for it is a necessary component of economic growth, i.e., that the settlers should be encouraged to maintain a personal endeavour towards higher productivity and economic expansion.

Continued productivity, and a high level of morale are both partly dependent upon permanence of settlement, and the promise of future ownership of the land which the families work. The resettled families would need to be given some assurance of security of tenure, ultimate ownership of land in the village, and assistance in the early months of their resettlement in the form of food and subsistence. (There are international food donors in the world today, such as the World Food Programme, based in Rome, which can assist such government-sponsored resettlement projects.)

The success of the entire programme of planned settlement will depend upon the extent and rate of capital formation in relation to the rate of capital input, and the number of persons settled on the land. The physical aspects of the settlement can be planned to procure optimum output from the available latent wealth; the community sites can be planned and located to provide the vital component of social cohesion which stimulates economic productivity; but, if the actual production cannot be satisfactorily marketed at its appropriate value, and satisfactory trade relations established through a proper system of selling the products both overseas and in the home markets, then the whole intention of such resettlement projects will be prejudiced. The settlers could end up with subsistence farming, which would generate insufficient wealth for continued expansion. The technical implementation of such resettlement projects needs to be based on market surveys of commodities which can be produced.

If such projects are undertaken under the management and financing of a government-owned stock-holding development company, then any contributions, services rendered, or investments made by the various government agencies, can be considered as being recoverable, and stock issued to each agency for the equivalent amount of capital outlay. In this way, the project is given the opportunity of amortizing itself, and national investment by each agency is recoverable to strengthen its own financial resources, and can be used for expanding its services either to new projects, or to the national development programme.

The emergence of more productive enterprises in the region would raise the overall living standards as well as the per capita productivity of the people in these rural areas.

The pioneer fringes of many of the developing nations today are invariably the source of the streams of city-bound rural migrants. By upgrading the manpower capacity of the people to develop the economy of the region themselves, by providing facilities for extending the infrastructure and means of communication within a total concept of regional development, and by providing also facilities for the marketing of the produce and financially backstopping the project of human settlement and development of natural resources, a situation of two-way economic benefit to the nation is created: a large segment of rural families refrain from swelling the continuing stream of migrants to the towns and cities, thereby easing the squatter problem there; and an increasing number of resident families in the region convert its latent economic resources into real wealth for both their own and the national economic benefit.

PLANNING RURAL-URBAN ADJUSTMENT AT THE NATIONAL LEVEL

The shifting rural-to-urban population throughout many countries of the world, with the resulting strain on the social and economic balances of the cities, is not without recognition among the governments of the world.

In July 1965, the Economic and Social Council of the United
Nations moved to resolve (Res. 1086, C. XXXI) that

> the U.N. should engage in carefully organized and co-ordinated
> research and training programmes to promote the modernization
> of both cities and countryside, and to minimize the undesirable
> effects of over-centralization of population, and of industries,
> through the development of improved patterns of human settle-
> ment and programmes of planned social and economic adjustment.

The way in which the problem can be met (if not totally,
then at least very considerably) is contained in the philosophy
of this resolution, by the three-pronged system of co-ordinated
research and training programmes, modernization of the existing
cities, and the establishment throughout the rural areas of a
totally new pattern of settlement. Each of the latter should be
planned to contain the essential elements of urban equipment,
educational facilities, convenient marketing, and cultural
associations, and built within a pattern of closer settlement. In
themselves, and coupled with adequate means of subsistence
and of generating wealth, and access to markets, they will act
as counter-attractions to the slum-squatter colonies of the cities.

By treating the problem on a proper *scientific basis,* and
establishing an accurate knowledge of the economic and social
trends (and balances) of the rapidly spreading towns and cities,
many of the governments of the afflicted areas would possess
the knowledge with which to readjust gradually those imbalances and avert the possible future decline of their cities
(and much unnecessary social conflict), through a planned
rural-urban distribution programme.

The need for new concepts of urban development for the
future, having regard to trends of urban economics, the potential for generating and redistributing wealth, and the minimum
criteria for decent urban living, is surely the challenge facing
the urban planners, designers, financiers, and administrators
of today.

The achievement of this end will involve the interdisciplinary
activity of the economic planners (versed in econometrics,
public finance, demograph, cost-benefit ratios of urban investment, promotion of trade, marketing and industry, planning
law and administration, etc.), the social planners (versed in

levels of living and the economic variables of social cohesion), together with the physical planners, the scientists, the land capability experts, and the economic geographers (who are versed in the development and economics of land use, settlement patterns, etc.). The patterns of settlement, and the physical possibilities of creating the environment (and the mechanics) for the continuity of a dynamic society on a regional basis can be quantitatively planned by governments, firstly as theoretical models, tested with pilot projects, then as long-range investment programmes designed and built into the national accounts system of the country.

In the high-density urbanized cities of Europe, the pressure of population on urbanized land over the years became more and more intense, until the concepts of urban design gradually changed from the classical monumental design inspired by the great Greek and Roman cities to a concept of cities planned and built within an organic and functional system. This trend has developed to the extent that complete new towns are being planned and built within a regional pattern. New towns of this type are being constructed in Great Britain and Russia and many other countries today.

However, for the capital deficient developing countries, where built-up urban land is at a premium, entirely new concepts in the form and function of urban centres and their interdependence with their hinterland need to be evolved. Models need to be designed for the quantitative investigation of the economic consequences of alternative use of land, and the multiple application of usable space, planned to provide higher density of living, with employment opportunities and incentives for higher productivity, and formation of capital. Advances in science and technology should be fully utilized, and the whole integrated to provide human and community living in a viable cohesive socio-economic activity. The economic progress of the town and city and their contribution to gross national productivity are matters of great significance. By means of any of the many methods available through persuasion and incentives, population can be redistributed throughout the land, and plans implemented to accelerate the rate of increase of national productivity. Methods of upgrading and applying human resources in the creation of both rural and urban wealth, and in the rationalization of urban living, have to be devised and inaugurated. Theoretical computer models for determining the programmes for measuring the variables involved are now becoming available, and can be put to use by governments of the developed world to facilitate the policies and decisions of the governments of the less developed nations.[7]

Urbanization policies, drawn from the determinants and consequences of population distribution, their productivity, wealth, and trends of social and economic behaviour, in relation to the variables of human response to investment programmes aimed at developing national resources, can be formulated now in a much more comprehensive way than ever was possible without the aid of electronic computers and data processing systems.

Even though these are still being developed, they have a present capacity which is more than adequate for the needs of the urbanization policies of governments in the developing world today.

In any national economic development concept, allocation of land uses within a co-ordinated programme of economic growth on a regional basis becomes an absolute necessity. The identification of the nodal points or polarity centres of economic growth and social progress, the distribution of capital formation enterprises among metropolitan cities, medium-sized towns, and small urban centres, and the determination of the optimum scale of settlements conducive to the economic growth and social advancement of the nation as a whole — these are among the several pre-investment investigations, the analysis of which

[7.] For a series of mathematical essays on "Rational Human Behaviour in a Social Setting", demonstrating the feasibility of applying econometrics to the rural-urban interdependence problem, and others, see Herbert A. Simon, *Models of Man* (New York: John Wiley and Sons, Inc., 1957), pp. 207–18. For other valuable references demonstrating the use of computers and the design of computer programmes for the beneficial use of society, see N. Weiner, *Human Use of Human Beings* (N.Y.: Avon Books, 1950). For an outline of the science of the control of communication processes, with the use of high-speed electronic processing of information, where information is treated as a statistical quantity, see N. Weiner, *Cybernetics* (Massachusetts: M.I.T. Press, 1948).

leads to policy decisions which form the basis and set the pattern for our future cities.

Governments are at a disadvantage in their policy and decision making if they do not have at their disposal a system for the comprehensive collation of data, and for processing and portraying this information in a meaningful way. The data collation and processing system should be designed to portray such relationships as the economic functioning of the various towns within the existing settlement pattern of a region. It is equally important that the government should be able to identify the various levels of living of the people throughout a region or the country in relation to their capacity for productivity, both quantitative and qualitative, or the flow of investment capital into the various towns or regions, identified on the basis of geographical location.

The information can now be collated (and needs to be collated) in such a way that all the essential components of urban life and its social and economic trends, variations, and interdependencies can be correlated and analyzed, not only as to subject matter, but as to geographical location, whether the subject is a village, a small town, or cities or regions in their spatial relationship with each other in the national frame of reference.[8]

However, designing a data processing programme for rural-urban analysis means programming for components which often, within their frame of spatial co-ordinates, are varying in relation to each other, because of prevailing policies and influences; the effects or consequences of an investment plan, incorporating the various components of productivity, trade and commerce, and the levels of living, for a given geographical region can now be predicted, provided there is an accurate measurement of human response to investment plans.

8. An interesting example of a Programme of Operations Research and Systems Analysis, designed for facilitating investment decision and policy making in the field of urban and rural development and housing and inter-related community development is to be found in the United Nations Special Fund assisted project for the National Housing Bank, Rio de Janeiro, Brazil. The Computer Data Service Centres, already established in most of the larger cities throughout the world, have an equipment configuration with a capacity adequate to store and process programmes of such a magnitude.

It is now possible to design a data processing system which can be used as a policy and decision making instrument for maintaining a better rural-urban balance in a country. It is complex, but not nearly so complex as some of the data processing involved in the space programme, or the design of modern supersonic aircraft. Attention, and much research finance amounting to hundreds of millions of dollars, have been devoted by governments and private organizations of the technologically advanced nations to using the very fast data processing capabilities of modern computers for solving these scientific problems. The computer "know-how" for the design of the flexible data processing programmes required for urbanization planning (the programmes could be valid for all countries) is now available.

Industry, transport, power, and settlement patterns, all operate and interact within the framework of a single set of spatial co-ordinates, and are the tools of planners for the implementation of the urbanization policy.[9]

Analysis of the data for national planning policy requires a computerized locational system. Our astronomers and ancient navigators have already provided the world with an accurate meridian system of co-ordinates, — latitudes and longitudes —

9.   For an interesting example of a comprehensive study of metro-politan growth, using locational co-ordinates, where the final displays do not appear as "maps" but as joint frequency distribution figures related to changing distances (a simple means of systematizing geographic data by reference to a standard "concentric rings" map, which does not need to be printed because of its simple geometry), see: D. Foley, R. Drake, D. Lyon, and B. Yuzenga, *Characteristics of Metropolitan Growth in California*, Vol. II (Berkeley: Centre for Planning and Development Research, University of California, December, 1965). For an example of computer synthesizing of large amounts of data for locating special functional areas, see: Robert C. Tryom, *Identification of Social Areas by Cluster Analysis* (University of California Press, 1955). See also Nicholas Negroponte and Leon Groisser, *Urban 5: An On-line Urban Design Partner* (Massachusetts Institute of Technology). This is a computer programme which can be used in a graphical display unit, directed at producing responsible urban architecture through the consideration of a multitude of salient, basic relationships.

universally used, and covering very accurately every country in the world. Every town, large or small, is already identified exactly by these positions recorded within the frame of one degree of latitude and one degree of longitude, approximately 60 nautical miles square at the equator, or a component section of "minutes" of the degree, equal to one nautical mile, or a component section of the "minute" of the degree, "the second", approximately 106 feet. *Manual* analysis and correlation of all the factors of urban data is a task so time-consuming, and so immense, requiring a skilled labour force which is just not available in the developing countries (or, in fact, in any country), that it has been unthinkable, previously, as a method for synthesizing urban growth data within a national frame of co-ordinates.

The data processing machines which are available today bring the whole of the analysis of rural-urban interdependence in a spatial co-ordinate control and identification system into the realm of reality. Comparative analysis and synthesis of information concerning the growth process of the selected town, or part of the town, spheres of influence, levels of living, unutilized yet potential exploitable resources, the value of capital formation which could be expected to result if developed according to a prescribed programme, and the consequential influences on other towns, i.e. the economic feasibility of such a proposed policy — all this information can be very quickly made available to the policy makers.

The existing circumstances of the settlement pattern of the whole country, big or small, can be synthesized, and the imbalances revealed graphically. The data can be stored on memory discs,[10] and later extracted and used to identify the trends of the various components.

Co-ordinate digitizers are now available to facilitate the location of every component of information concerning town or countryside in its geographical setting, for each item of information can be recorded with a co-ordinate identification of a "unit area" directly (degrees, minutes, seconds). The digitizing machine accepts the map references as input.

[10.] "Random access disc files" are most suited for storing the information for speedy extraction and correlation.

Electronic graphical portrayal of the processed data is also very advanced. Systems of graphically portraying the data on Graphical Display Units, using cathode screens which display the results of the most complex mathematical computations in chart or graph form for immediate visual analysis, giving a ready interpretation of statistics, trends, and indices, are already available commercially. With the use of a "Light Pen", various alternative proposals concerned with policy and decision making can be plotted directly onto the screen, and, through a "feed-back" mechanism for the information, the consequences in many related fields of investment or levels of living, or in planning proposals, can be revealed quantitatively.

What the data computers will not do is make the final decisions for the policy makers; they, the policy makers, represent the "General Will" of the "collective moral person", the government. The system enunciated above only delivers the information accurately and speedily to the policy makers, to ensure that a comprehensive picture of the affairs of the nation is quickly available to facilitate the production of more effective decisions and programmes of action.

The scientific equipment which can thus facilitate the making of policy decisions aimed at attaining a more equitable distribution of population throughout the land is now available for use by governments to serve the cause of humanity.

PART THREE

Conclusion

CHAPTER SIX

Conclusion and Summary

GENERAL REVIEW

The evidence available indicates that the roots of urban squatting are to be found deep in moral and social philosophy, and that, as a recognizable phenomenon, it is an essential by-product of society, related directly to the economic rate of growth of a town or city. In this sense, it is a component of city evolution.

The towns and cities have a spatial relationship within an established hierarchy of settlement across the country, which should be interdependent with the rural settlement pattern, within a national framework of social and economic development. Though rural-to-urban migration has been a behavioural trend throughout history, urban squatting reveals the inability or incapacity of the present urban structure of many of the developing nations to absorb the shift of population from the rural environment to the towns and cities; it focuses attention on the ever widening imbalance in the living standards of rural dwellers and town dwellers.

The cities of Europe had to face the same problem in the seventeenth and eighteenth centuries; whether the proportion of squatters to established citizenry in the European cities of the eighteenth century was the same as that in the developing nations today is not known, but in any case the cities of Europe were expanding within the global pattern of trade and the industrial system which they themselves had created; they were cities in a developing world then, just as the cities in Latin America, Asia, Africa, and the Middle East are today.

Where, then, are the criteria which distinguish a "developing" nation from a "developed" one? When does a country cease to be a "developing" nation and come under the "developed" category?

The terms "developed world" and "developing or underdeveloped world" have come into common usage particularly since the creation of the United Nations Organization. In general, they are used to denote the difference between countries which have attained certain prescribed average levels of living, and countries which have not attained those levels, though the dichotomy between the two is expressed or defined more by the difference in the level of human fertility than by any other criterion. [1]

The system for quantitatively measuring the levels of living has been devised by the United Nations Research Institute for Social Development, Geneva, and can be used as a universal system. The comparison of these levels has not been established for all the countries of the world because the "national account statistics for many countries are not available in comparative form, nor is it possible to compare acceptable purchasing power parity". [2]

The system devised is for the quantitative measurement of levels of living through the component indices of nutrition, housing, education, leisure, security, and surplus; these figures are then related as three main groups of component indices: physical, cultural, and surplus. The information is then synthesized into a comparative national index, which can be used for national comparisons. Of the twenty countries studied to demonstrate the system, the levels of living varied from an index of 181.8 for one country to 40.8 for another. The report gives the warning, however, that it is not possible yet to "conclude from the pilot study that the average level of living

[1.] See footnote 1, chapter 1.
[2.] Drewnowski and Scott, *The Level of Living Index* (United Nations Research Institute for Social Development, Report No. 4 [Geneva, September 1966]), Table 2, pp. 60–68.

in the world is equal to the average of the 20 countries, or
that the distribution of levels of living is the same for the
world generally as it is for the 20 countries". [3]

It can be conceded, however, that there is sufficient information available from various sources throughout the world
today for it to be possible to draw up a general classification
for all countries. The list could classify the countries, ranging
from those which have attained high standards of living, and
whose productivity and trading activities provide a surplus
sufficient to sustain those levels, to those countries whose
capital-formating capacity is inadequate to stimulate sufficient
productivity to meet the increasing needs of their ever increasing
population. All this is quantifiable, and therefore can constitute
the basis of a planned programme of international assistance.

Just as there exists today much speculation on the possible
improvement of society, so it was in the eighteenth century.
Malthus, among others, came to the conclusion that inequalities
in the levels of living could never be reduced, unless unutilized
land was brought under cultivation annually to match the
subsistence needs of the increasing population. He also saw the
fallacy of the "inquiry of Dr. Adam Smith" into the nature and
causes of the wealth of nations, in that the economic philosophy
of Dr. Smith made no acknowledgement of the needs of the
poor of the country, nor did it provide any basis on which
they could be supported.

Just as there were violent fluctuations in the economic
stability of the countries relying upon the economic philosophy
of Dr. Smith, culminating in the global financial crisis of the
1930's, so one can expect much the same to happen to the
social and economic stability of the cities of the developing
world, where the established authorities make inadequate
provision for the growing number of poor.

In the developing world, many of the city authorities do not
have the resources, either of skilled manpower or finances, nor
do they have the administrative capacity to undertake the
technical task of integrating the urban squatters; some do not
even have any policy on urbanization; some are so underdeveloped that the prescribed minimum levels of urban living

3. *Ibid.*

are still far beyond their economic means, and any foreseeable possibility of attainment. In most cases in the developing nations, the consolidation of the collective expression of the nation in its cities, and the recognition that these cities should be developed as the centres of highest organizational capacity in order to develop the economic strength of the nation, are being frustrated by the increasingly heavy burden imposed by the inflow from rural and provincial areas of poverty-stricken in-migrants whose labour cannot be made productive, since there is no industrial or employment system to absorb them.

As a means of reducing the crippling economic fluctuations of the early twentieth-century world, John Maynard Keynes saw a necessity for the various governments of Europe and North America to take a firmer control of the monetary flow systems throughout their respective countries. Similarly, Charles Abrams sees a necessity for the national governments of the developing world to take a firmer control over the urbanization process in their countries. (He even considers that the United States ought to adopt a new philosophy towards its cities.)

The economic growth of a nation is dependent to a large extent upon the stability and strength of its cities. Yet, the very growth of the huge squatter problem that is spreading around, in, and throughout the cities of the developing world leads one to believe that an inadequate urban philosophy has been adopted by many of the governments concerned.

Many governments throughout the world have recognized a malignancy in the urban squatter problem, and programmes of action of several different types, seven of which have been described in this book, have been evolved, and some actually put into effect. Nevertheless, the sum total of the effectiveness of the programmes, so far, is so negligible as to have made very little impression on the total problem, except perhaps in places such as Israel, Hong Kong, or Singapore. The combined allocation of resources from both national and local governments, and the substantial charitable contribution from non-government agencies, are not even containing the present number of squatters within the existing colonies; even less has been accomplished in meeting the challenge of what is believed to be part of the cause — the low living standards in the rural areas.

The dimension of the social and economic problem looming up before the cities of the developing nations can be better understood if it is realized that the increase of population over the decade 1950–1960 nearly equalled the estimated total world population during the seventeenth century, i.e. approximately 500 million people. The reality of the challenge which the government and municipal administrations of the developing nations have to face is contained in the fact that, over the next *forty years,* the world population of 1960, of nearly 3,000 million, is expected to increase to more than 7,000 million,[4] and the *urban* population of all the developing nations is expected to *increase more than five-fold* to 5,255 million persons, i.e. well over 50 per cent of the total.

If all this urban population is to be accommodated at the existing levels of living, the urban settlements will have to be extended and built to five times their present dimensions. Without some new concepts of urban design and construction to suit the needs of the developing nations, this would present a demand for capital outlay of at least five times the existing total urban investment, which, in many cases, represents an accumulation of capital investment spanning as much as two hundred years. This would appear to be unrealistic, as matters stand at present. The regions particularly affected are in Asia and the Far East, the Middle East, some parts of Africa and the Mediterranean, and the whole of Latin America.

It is patently obvious that the present pattern of urban settlements throughout the rural areas of the various nations is hopelessly inadequate to absorb the increasing rural population. The result is that instead of the population of the country growing within a hierarchy of settlement related directly to the population-supporting capacity of the land, with the urban settlements supporting the needs of, and being interdependent with, the agricultural working population, the rural surpluses are gravitating into the towns that do exist, and threatening to weaken and destroy the economic foundations and social stability of those towns, and, therefore, of the nation as a whole.

As the United Nations demographers have demonstrated,[5] the urban dwellers of the developing world are soon to consti-

4. See Table B in chapter 1.
5. See p. 17 and Table C in chapter 1.

tute the great majority of urban dwellers throughout the whole world; but most of them, as the situation stands at present, will be urban squatters, who, once in a position of dominance, will represent in themselves a "collective moral person", and will then represent the "General Will" — of the towns they inhabit, in particular.

If they have not been educated in the essentials of town management, operation, repair, and maintenance, they may possess control of the cities, but they will not possess the knowledge with which to prevent the decay and ultimate collapse of these same cities. The very structure on which the expansion of the nation's economy depends will be weakened.

The challenge of the growth of urban squatting throughout the cities of the developing nations calls for mobilization of the total resources of mankind on an international scale of operations to assist these smitten cities to carry their burden. The social, human, and economic forces now being generated in many of the cities are forces of deprivation which can be adjusted by timely government action based on the scientific method and planned urban development throughout the entire nation.

The real challenges facing the national planners are the finding of a method which will encourage an increase in individual productivity, and the utilization of that productivity to create, and equitably distribute, the increased wealth throughout the land.

The challenge of organizing the production of food concentrate or foodstuff to double its quantity within the next thirty years is not beyond the organizational capacity of man on a scientific and technological basis, but the governmental organization needed for its production and distribution requires much more comprehensive national planning than is being employed at present; the necessary adjustment of the complex balance of payment will require considerable international collaboration. Nearly 50 per cent of the people of the world today have a nutrient intake which is less than the recommended average; thousands still die of famine annually in several parts of the world, and in some countries in the Far East even the government-subsidized rice is too expensive for the great majority of the poor.

There is no shortage of land on which the old historical growth of settlements could proceed; if planned, and if planned properly, the excessive concentration of a disproportionately increasing number of poor in the existing cities of wealth could be avoided; what is absent is the programmed rationalized use of the nation's land for agricultural, grazing, forestry, recreation, park, and game reserves, and a hierarchy of urban structure throughout the land, whereby inequalities in living standards are greatly reduced, and easy access to urban facilities is provided for most people in rural areas.

As the scientific method was applied by the entrepreneurs and governments of Europe and North America to control economic conditions, and provide for the continuous progress of their society, so the time has come to employ the scientific method to evaluate the resources of the various developing nations — their human resources, physical resources, and potential economic resources — and to utilize the process of diagnosis, synthesis, and planning (evolved over the past century into a recognizable method by Patrick Geddes) along with the mechanical devices and instruments now available to store, extract, correlate, analyze, and synthesize data on a scale of operation and at a speed never before possible, for the planning and implementation of national rural-urban inter-dependent development.

Without such a conscious urbanization programme on the part of the governments, by which the multiplying population from both the rural and urban centres can be readjusted throughout the land in a hierarchy of settlement based on the economic supporting capacity of the land and the social balance of settlements, then migrating rural families must continue to swell the existing urban squatter colonies in the existing cities.

SUMMARY OF THE HISTORICAL TREND

The notions of adjusting the social and economic imbalances of the rural-urban scene, of diagnosing the ills of a city, of upgrading manpower capacity in order to increase productivity, of consciously adjusting the urban environment to promote the development of a higher moral fibre and character among the poor, are by no means new. Quantitative analysis of demographic trends and their effect on the future of society is not confined to the scientific techniques of the twentieth century, but rather originated in the late eighteenth century in Europe. Thomas Malthus was the first to give the scholars of Europe a proper scientific basis for the study of demography. It is unknown whether Malthus was in any way influenced by the writings of Rousseau, though it is possible, because his father was closely associated with Rousseau; it is equally possible that his experience with the East India Company, as Professor of Modern History and Political Economy in the college of the company, provided some stimulus for his thesis.

Because of his personal reaction to the rapidly growing urban society of the late eighteenth century, Rousseau saw a close connection between the structure of society and the moral and psychological condition of the individual. Even in his day, he believed that the mounting discord and moral confusion of urban society was the inescapable consequence of excessive inequalities of wealth, and the complexity and growing size of the cities. His view was that in a vast community with a complex economy, there must inevitably be a hierarchy and inequality, a situation where a great majority of passive citizens are controlled and exploited by an active few, unless positive action is taken by the people to correct the imbalance through a new "social contract".

He contended that man cannot be on good terms with his neighbour, nor achieve personal dignity or a sense of liberty, except in a community simple enough to be intelligible to himself, and simple enough to enable him to take a full and equal part in government.

His ideal was the creation of a series of small egalitarian states throughout Europe, but this was based on a social theory only, and denied the economics of land use; it took no cognizance of the geographical aspects of the supporting capacity of various types of soils, or of the location of the towns in relation to the commercial or trade flow lines.

The very visible increase of population in the towns and cities of Europe in the late eighteenth century was construed by Malthus as the result of an increasing birth rate, whereas in fact it marked the beginning of the decline in the urban death rate. His principles are particularly valid and pertinent today for the developing nations, and his theories are in fact a contribution to the solution of the twentieth-century problem, because in most of the developing nations, though the birth rate is increasing, and the death rate declining still further, food production is not increasing annually at a rate comménsurate with demand and need.

Contemporary with Malthus was Robert Owen, who demonstrated that "industrialism" and "urbanism" could be, in proper combination, the means towards the continued socio-economic improvement of society; his thesis was that such a combination could be the means of continuing to provide good standards of living for the increasing population, the essential social aspects of growth and development, as well as the economic aspects. His proposal was that the government should encourage the establishment of agro-industrial villages throughout the land on a planned basis.

Owen contended that man's character, in its natural state, is formed by circumstances over which he has no control; therefore, conversely, it is possible to influence the development of a man's character by providing a specific environment during his early years. When in 1790, at the age of nineteen, he took over the responsibility for the New Lanark Mills, he found the living conditions of the workers so poor, the housing so inadequate, and the people so demoralized because of the neglect of education and sanitation, that crime and vice were flourishing. He began by improving their homes, and mainly by his own personal influence had the people trained in habits of order, cleanliness, and thrift; he provided stores at which only good-quality articles could be purchased at near cost price; the sale of liquor was controlled; and education was provided for the young.

As a measure to counteract the urban pauperism in his day, he proposed that the Government should undertake a social experiment and create several small agro-industrial communities, with a population of 1,000 to 3,000 persons in each. Owen carried his notions of resettlement further, and proposed that the community as a whole, under government supervision, should have more influence over the children than the parents, and that the community should be collectively owned and operated. For those who cherished their family and religion, this notion was, and still is, offensive. As subsequent social experiments were to reveal (and as Owen was to learn from his own private experiment in America many years later, when he lost four-fifths of his fortune in such a project), the success of such projects depends upon a high level of social cohesion, mutual confidence amongst the families, a community endowed with many different skills and resourcefulness, and the right always of individual liberty of thought and security of tenure.

Though his total concept was not acceptable in his time, his ideal and demonstration of upgrading the human resources of the families, his provision of a firm economic base for the community, his limiting of economic profit, and his reinvestment of capital gains in the balanced social development of the community stand as a particularly valuable example for what is needed in the twentieth-century towns and cities of the developing world.

However, the society of his age had not acknowledged that there was any organic form to a city, nor that it contained any dynamics of its own form, but rather that it was built in the form of classical beauty, for the convenience of established society. The grottos and garrets were out of sight and out of mind.

Throughout Europe, then, urban problems were mounting visibly, as they are in the developing countries of the world today. But in Europe industrialism, coupled with global trading and finance, provided the means of economic expansion to meet the social and economic demands of the urbanism of that day. There were many social imbalances, but, over the nineteenth and into the early part of the twentieth century, these were gradually adjusted. In the developing nations, however, the medium which will enable the cities of today and tomorrow to generate wealth at a geometric rate to match the growth of population has yet to be established.

The first to begin the scientific identification of the social and economic factors on which the behaviour and trends of a city depend, and the relationship between family and town, was Frédéric Pierre Guillaume Le Play, a French mining engineer.

Le Play began to evolve a scientific method for quantifying the family-city relationship; he began always from the datum point of the family budget for various levels of society. His studies then extended to cover the relationship between the workers and industry, and then the relationship between industry and the total population. He laid the basis for quantitatively examining the relationship between rural and urban society, and for the social and economic hierarchy of urban society.

This, however, covered only part of the urban scene, for there is also an essential physical and biological force in all urban growth and expansion, particularly in its evolutionary process, as it grows from a small village or small town to the size of a large town or large city; the growth takes shape in relation to other communities, all bearing a spatial relation, one to the other, in a regional setting. This had not been defined previously, and therefore could not be related in the same quantitative dimension of measurement as that of the social and economic factors.

During part of his education in Paris, Patrick Geddes, in 1879, came into direct contact with the theories of Le Play; he saw in the city an essential biological structure. By extending the work and principles of Le Play, and by utilizing the biological laws governing the behaviour and response patterns of the individual, he evolved an acceptable scientific method for diagnosing a town or city in its regional environment. This method has since been used as the basis for modern-day civic and regional planning. It involves basically a process of diagnosis, analysis, and synthesis of all the factors related to urban growth and development. He was able to demonstrate that the development of human communities was essentially based on a biological process; therefore, the remedy for urban sickness would depend upon an accurate diagnosis of the complex interrelation between people, their environment, and their activities.

Although the present trend of urban squatting throughout modern-day cities in the developing nations gives every cause for deep concern, the members of government, the public administrators, and the professional consultants and advisers to all the governments afflicted with the problem have at their disposal the benefit of a scientific method evolved over 150 years of experience in Europe. From this system can be drawn a method for the diagnostic survey, analysis, synthesis, and projection of the trends of the various sectors of urban growth, and from it remedial legislative and economic measures can be introduced to correct the present widening human, economic, and social imbalances of so many towns and cities in the world today.

A system for quantitatively identifying levels of living on a comparative basis, not only town to town within a region, but nation to nation, has been devised by the United Nations Research Institute in Geneva. Now it is possible to measure the dimension of the total problem of the inequalities of rural-urban levels of living, town by town, district by district, region by region, and register all items of information accurately, as they are contained in their physical or geographical location, identified by their spatial co-ordinates, preferably, latitude and longitude, or parts thereof, and recorded in data processing machines which have adequately large storage capacity. From these, for the purpose of comparative analysis and diagnosis, the composite information can be retrieved with a speed which has never been possible previously. It is on this basis that the policy makers of the governments concerned have at their disposal the scientific method and the modern-day instruments with which to meet the urban squatter problem of the developing world; the application of these now needs to be guided by the moral and social philosophy of humanitarianism.

The organizational capacity of man has proved capable of meeting many a challenge before this century; surely, it will be able to rise to this challenge also. There must obviously be some changes in the present structure of urban society and in the existing sense of values. The majority of towns and cities in the developing nations are now in the process of a social transformation; what the carapace of their late-twentieth-century cities will be, it is difficult to predict, because organized urban society still has time to "alter the stream of events"[6] and assist in dealing with the fungus, before the plague is let loose.

6. The phrase is Charles Abrams', from *The City Is the Frontier* (New York: Harper and Row, 1967).

APPENDICES

Notes on the Design of a Preliminary Urban Data Collation System on Which Comparative Trends of Urbanization for the Various Towns and Cities Could Be Analyzed

The urbanization policy must ultimately include a ratio between urban and rural population, and the pattern within which population should be distributed among the towns, cities, and rural hinterlands; this needs to be based on natural population and the economic supporting capacity of the land, if the region is to progress socially and economically in a balanced way. Scientific knowledge of the land-capability makes this possible. Optimum economic and social utilization of land has to be determined quantitatively, if it is to serve as the basis for an urbanization programme.

The capacity of the city to absorb the ever increasing stream of migrants from the rural areas, and the extent of national government investment necessary to maintain proper urban standards in the cities, can, and must be identified, if the economy is to continue to progress.

Such economic analysis and formulae provide the frame within which planners can prepare budgets for housing and industrialization on a valid basis, particularly in relation to the distribution of settlement in its geographical setting; it is within such programmes that the urban squatter problem can be assimilated.

It is the design of the flexible system of data collation, processing, and correlation which is important at this stage, for it must be compre hensive enough to embrace ultimately all the component parts of urban living, identifying the functions of the smaller towns as well as the large cities.

As a start, for the developing nations, the information can be collated at an accurate but general level, rather than in excessive detail. When this has been displayed to give the national characteristics, the second stage of detailed level of information is recorded for geographical regions or districts, until, over the years, the process of collating the data in a prescribed form through locally established offices and agencies becomes a naturally accepted procedure.

Most of the information which would be required for a national comparative study of existing conditions, and the analysis for regional decisions, is always available through some office of the local administration or from some private organization in the community itself. It is a matter of arranging for its assembly within a prescribed and designed programme. The information can be assembled under the following headings as a first step in the "national scan" of each town:

1. Demographic Characteristics, Levels of Living, and Housing Conditions

The trends of population growth rate should be tabulated over the period from 1900, or as far back as possible, and the consistency of trends of population growth and spread of land use identified for its application in projecting the destiny of present trends.

It is also necessary to note the ratio of male to female and the structure of the various age groups of the urban population; the census offices of most governments in the world today carry out this work, but it needs to be plotted for each town.

The spread of settlement and actual use of land can be measured from land-use survey maps (and, if possible, confirmed from air-photo-mosaics). (See item 2.) From this same information, a map should be compiled to show the density of settlement, and multiple uses for different areas, and the location of the squatters, *favelados, mocambos*, etc.

The trend of increase of squatter population needs to be plotted on the population graph, and on the maps.

The income structure of each town needs to be compiled

from records of sales, market transactions, value of productivity, and employment structure; this is invariably held by the City Fiscal, who needs the information for tax purposes. It is also necessary to compile data on the various living standards of the citizens, as well as of the squatters, specifically in relation to health and nutrition,[1] accommodation, environmental sanitation, etc; the dimension and trend of the social and human problem of the squatter colonies must be identified if a programme of action is to be drawn up.

The characteristics of the housing situation in the town can usually be extracted from the census office; the United Nations has already contributed much to improving the census systems throughout the developing nations. Up-to-date information on building licenses issued and buildings actually constructed can usually be obtained from the office of the city engineer, or mayor, though it is conceded that this may be lacking in accuracy.

The living conditions of the town need to be noted; information on such matters as seasonal variations of temperature, hazards (such as floods, typhoons, etc.) need to be included, for all can be related to normal comfort conditions, and may well indicate reasons for loss of economic progress.

2. LAND-USE CHARACTERISTICS

These can be plotted on a cadastral map of convenient size and by the use of spatial co-ordinates can be computerized, as previously described. There is a method of land-use surveys which is now in almost universal use.

For towns of up to 100,000 population, sufficient information on which decisions and policies can be formulated for preliminary purposes can be obtained from a "windscreen survey", i.e. the observer plots the information directly onto the maps from observations made through the windscreen of his car, and confirmed, where possible, by air photographs or cadastral maps. The various areas of land use can then be computed from the map, or measured with a planimeter.

[1.] See Drewnowski and Scott, *The Level of Living Index* (United Nations Research Institute for Social Development, Report No. 4 [Geneva, September 1966]).

Graphical portrayal of the information on maps of convenient size quickly reveals any uneconomic spread of settlement. This in turn warns of the likelihood of having to incur disproportionate expenditure on the extension of the infrastructure and public utilities to service the uncontrolled spread.

A map of equal size should be compiled showing the general physical characteristics of the site of the town, drainage lines, areas liable to flooding, good-quality soil areas, and suitable land for the extension of the settlement.

A map of equal size should also be compiled to illustrate the current commercial value of land throughout the various sectors of the city. This information can be portrayed graphically in the form of "iso- valuation" lines, extracted from information obtained from the Land Tax Assessor's Office. This map is important, as Land Tax is usually a most significant source of income for the city, and any discrepancies between actual value and assessed value will soon be made clear.

3. Productivity, Employment, Capital Investment

Information on the productivity, employment structure, and capital formation of the town is vital. A table can be compiled showing the number of persons employed, and the categories of employment. This can usually be obtained from the City Fiscal or City Treasurer, with whom all places of employment should be registered. The most convenient categories under which to list the various types of employment are:

Home employment and personal services
Professional services — doctors, attorneys, architects, etc.
Finance and banking — accountants, auditors, etc.
Commercial and marketing
Building construction
Manufacturing — light, heavy, medium
Storage
Transport
Public and essential services
   Health,
   Education,
   Public utilities, etc.
Amusement and hotels
Mining, agriculture, fishing, and others

By using a "co-ordinate identification of unit area" of land for any town or community, it is possible to correlate the use of the land, and its percentage relationship within a specific classification of use (similar to the list above), with the value of productivity and types of employment that are carried out on that unit area of land. By an extension of this "comparative information" system to cover all the communities, towns, and cities of the nation, it is possible to draw out an assessment of the variation in the economic efficiency of the urban structure, on a nationwide comparative basis.

The table provides a simple method for direct correlation, and an analysis of the urban economic structure of the various towns in such a way that comparisons can be made for towns within the region, inter-regionally, and on a national basis. Gross densities, the extent of spread of settlement, the value of productivity, and the infrastructure to be provided can be analyzed directly in relation to the city budget; the source of income for the town administration and the sources of income for the whole town can be measured and identified, and policy decisions can be made at national and local government levels to adjust imbalances or, alternatively, to identify specific localities which need more capital investment to raise prevailing standards.

The value of production for the various sectors of the cities is invariably available from the local Chamber of Commerce, and/or industry. Similarly, the trends and activities of local sales, trade, and market should be available from the same source, and from this information the trends of the average per capita purchasing power of the town can be estimated.

Information on the city budget, sources of income for city expenditure, etc. are always available from the office of the Prefectura or Fiscal.

Details of the extent of paved and unpaved roads, storm-water drainage canals, and sewerage lines, the capacity of the sewerage treatment plant, the source, quantity, and capacity of the water supply, the source, distribution, and unit costs of the power supply, the river, port, and harbour facilities are all usually in the possession of the Office of the Mayor or the City Engineer, and a unit cost related to each is also available for estimating purposes. The information can be plotted out on maps of the same dimension as the land use and settlement spread maps. Information on the system, efficiency, and regularity of refuse disposal should be available from the local health officer.

The standards of the levels of living, and any discrepancies between the spread of settlement, the infrastructure and public services, the productive capacity and purchasing power of the residents, can be revealed by a correlation and analysis of this information.

For each town in its regional setting, the means of communication — telephone, radio-telephone, postal service, heavy transport (rail, ship, or road), and air transport — need to be clearly described and graphically portrayed.

When the programme has been designed, and the local authorities have been orientated and trained in the system of collating the data, it should be possible to verify trends of urban behaviour throughout the country every twelve months; many items will not change, but changes and their possible influence can be identified quickly by the government.

Ultimately, and as an aid in policy decision making by the government in dealing with the above housing and urbanization problems, an accurate and quantitative record of the resources of the building industry, and its distribution throughout the country, will be necessary. This can usually be best undertaken in collaboration with the Building Contractors' Associations of the country; the amount of skilled labour available to the building industry, the stock of materials held, the rate of production and the source of materials, can all be tabulated and related to each town or region.

From an analysis of the national inventory of the urbanization process (expressed in terms of resources, human, capital, potential capital generating), one can determine quantitatively the extent of urbanization which any particular developing nation can actually support within its own national economic rate of progress, measured against its levels of productivity and capital accumulation capacity. National policies and decisions can then be formulated therefrom. The forces and patterns of urbanization on investments and returns, capital formation, the social profile, environmental health, the aesthetics of physical development, and the urban economic structure —

all need to be evaluated and quantitatively analyzed as a basis for stimulating national economic progress, and arriving at capital formation targets made necessary today in the developing nations by the need to sustain excessively increasing numbers of presently uneconomic urban squatters in the established cities.

Once the information is synthesized and correlated within prescribed standards of levels of living, the need for remedial action by direct or indirect pre-investment activity by local, state, or national government is revealed.

Provision of the financial resources needed for the upgrading of manpower resources can also be determined. Programmes which are planned and designed to strengthen the agrarian economy, by the resettlement of many of the families throughout a region within a pattern of land utilization which is consciously planned to provide the settlers with optimum economic progress, and in which the families undertake the construction and development of much of their new communities through self-help techniques, can also be considered valid alternatives. The prize of ultimately owning their own land in a respectable, well-organized urbanized community in an agrarian setting is in itself a major attraction and incentive for a large proportion of squatters, and this motivation can be quantified in the sum total of the resettlement programme, and the cost-benefit ratio in the national economic scene determined.

The objective of any urbanization programme is to make the cities more efficient (not only for the present but for the mounting population of the future); the programme needs to be viable and feasible within the limits of permissible conditions of economic progress and the administrative organizational capacity.

This cannot be accomplished by statutes alone, or by building by-laws, or zoning ordinances, which are invariably twenty years out of date; these are but the instruments, not the indicators, which are used to achieve the ends of the urbanization policy. The decisions which provide for the future improvement of our society still rest with man himself.

Summary of Procedure Which Can Be Used for Identifying and Quantifying the Squatter Problem of a Town

Once the boundaries of the squatter colonies have been identified, their exact location can be plotted on a cadastral map, and plotted in relation to existing urban land use, the present settlement spread of the city, and proposed future land uses. Whether it is possible to "recuperate" the squatter colony on its present site and gradually assimilate the residents into the established urban scene, or whether they should be relocated in an "urban" village, in low-income housing projects, or rural relocation projects, will become evident, and a systematic programme of action, the allocation of budgetary and city resources, and the recruitment of voluntary services, can be prescribed.

A Preliminary Survey

The scope of the preliminary survey in and around each squatter colony can be classified under five main headings — physical, social, economic, administrative, and political:

Physical

(I) Plot out on maps the existing lines of all public services, water supply, drainage, sewerage, electricity, etc., and any proposed extension of services which is likely to affect the locality.

(II) Plot out on maps the contours, natural drainage lines, extent of surrounding catchment area, and direction and system of run-off and disposal of surface water; check the site for liability to flooding.

(III) Identify the ownership of land, and any reserved uses, or ancient monuments, etc. which have to be preserved.

Social

(IV) Identify and plot on maps all communal and social facilities, including hospitals, churches, schools, etc., which are directly accessible to the locality.

(V) Carry out a survey to identify the social character of the locality; this can be related to the land use proposed in a master-plan concept.

Economic

(VI) Establish the economic character of the squatter locality in its own content — sources of income, rent-paying capacity, purchasing power of the inhabitants, their productive capacity — and also the economic character of the site master-plan; this should include information on any planned centres for shopping, culture, recreation, etc.

Administrative

(VII) Examine the building by-laws and regulations applicable to the locality, the permissible densities of occupation and land use, fire gradings of structure, light, air, space about buildings, and draw out an analysis of strong and durable structures which have an acceptable level of accommodation.

Political

(VIII) Identify any obvious political or personal loyalty alignment which the majority of the existing residents may have, and the hierarchy of leadership which exists, and which could collaborate in any proposed improvement project.

If the results of the study indicate that the locality is suited for public low-cost housing for residential or mixed residential purposes, a "diagnosis" of the locality is justified, to determine the existing levels and conditions of living of the present occupants and the extent of rehabilitation necessary. This information can be synthesized with the norms of standards of redevelopment envisaged in:

(a) the master-plan concept of the city; and
(b) the locality itself.

Detailed Survey of Squatter Colony

An adequate diagnosis of a squatter colony depends upon an equally adequate *inventory of the locality*.

The information is best collated by a team of community surveyors — one responsible for soil and engineering aspects; one responsible for the social survey and household interviews; one responsible for all the economic aspects of the families, and the productivity of the individuals throughout the colony; and one responsible for the health and medical aspects of the families, and the environmental sanitation aspects. The following is a useful guide to the information which needs to be collated, but specific localities may require the collation of additional data, according to the specific local circumstances.

The detailed information should be plotted on convenient-scale cadastral maps of the locality under study. From the information plotted and analyzed, a programme of action, and an estimate of costs can be determined, based on a proposed design covering relocation of families, engineering and construction works, social facilities, health facilities, buildings and staff, and possibly some employment opportunities.

Physical data

(a) Plot and identify existing land uses contiguous with the squatter site, and the squatter site itself, employing a colour notation for the various uses, such as residential, commercial, industrial (light or heavy), parks and play areas, schools and educational establishments, buildings for community purposes, hospitals and clinics, roads and public land, government buildings and land, etc. Each area of specific use should be measured and related as a percentage of the total land use. Much has been published concerning the percentage relationship of urban land uses, for many towns throughout the world, and these references can be used as a basis of comparison for economic uses. The various existing structures can be related to the master-plan for any conforming uses; if no statutory master-plan exists, then some of the more permanent structures could be incorporated in a proposed redesign.

(b) Subsoil conditions and bearing capacity of the soil need to be determined, along with existing public service lines, such as stormwater drainage, sewerage, water supply, electricity lines.

(c) Note age and condition of all existing structures. For residential buildings, soundness of structure, types of materials (permanent and durable or impermanent and makeshift), number of rooms, types of rooms, light, air and ventilation to the various houses, the sanitation arrangements, systems of waste disposal, laundry and drying areas, sizes of rooms, sizes of buildings, and sizes of lots need to be identified and plotted; for industrial or commercial or other buildings, soundness and life of structure, usable space, and sizes of lots need to be plotted. The extent of the obsolescence of the structures needs to be identified, for this gives some idea of the cost of replacement.

(d) Contours of the land, and details of the provisions which have been made for drainage and disposal of surface run-off need to be noted, along with any areas liable to flooding.

(e) Note any high tension power transmission lines through or adjacent to the site.

(f) Note existing conditions of all road surfaces.

(g) Check the micro-climate of the location; e.g., any tendency to fog, sulphur-fumes from nearby chimneys, or nearby noxious industries, or any peculiarities of climate and temperature changes which affect the health of the inhabitants.

(h) Check any nuisance factors, such as broken or blocked drains, noisy or noxious industries affecting the residents.

(i) Where applicable, site coverage, floor space index, and heights of buildings should be noted.

(j) Check general visual aesthetics of the locality.

The human content

Social data

(Much of this can be portrayed graphically.)

(a) Note occupancy rate and density of buildings; for residential buildings identify the number of persons per habitable room per structure; for industrial or commercial use, identify the number of persons employed. All the above should be related to the sizes of rooms in item (c) of Physical Data.

(b) Make analysis of family structure throughout locality, including the size of family, age structure, any evidence of the "extended family" in one household, or doubling-up of families in one household, occupational aptitudes, actual family income, levels of skills and earning capacity, and whether these are being harnessed and used productively.

(c) Plot out separately all educational, communal, social, and recreational buildings and areas of land, and the extent to which they are used or are effective; also their structural condition, and the personnel manning such centres. Identify the number of doctors, priests, and social and community workers who are working with the people of the squatter colony.

(d) Plot out home recreational facilities, such as radios, T.V. Identify also stoves, refrigerators, and other such utilities, for each residence.

(e) Identify any culturally homogeneous groups throughout the colony.

(f) Identify levels of health and nutrition for the population throughout the locality.

(g) Determine any migratory tendencies, into or away from the locality over the past five years, along with the origin of the resident families immediately prior to their taking up residence in the squatter colony.

(h) Determine the extent of existing group organizations within the locality, the leadership patterns and the harmony of association of the various social groups, and any noticeable social stratification.

(i) Determine cultural aspirations and attitudes of families.

Economic circumstances

(Much of this information can also be plotted graphically.)

(a) Identify the legal title-holder of the land.

(b) Note land values of existing properties surrounding the colonies. Plot the iso-valuation lines on cadastral map, if possible.

(c) Determine family income, in relation to cost of living, and family budgeting, the proportion of income actually spent on shelter, and make an estimate of the possible outlay on shelter.

(d) For those employed, determine the distance and time for journey to work, and how much of the family budget is used for travelling.

(e) Note employment skills, and trade skills amongst the families in each colony, the extent of employment or productivity of each worker, their aptitudes and the utilization of their aptitudes for increased economic productivity.

(f) The extent to which public services are provided at present should be noted, along with the payment capacity of families for such services.

(g) The extent of car ownership should also be noted.

(h) Estimates of value of residential structures can be made, and a decision made as to whether they are sufficiently strong to be preserved or should be demolished. This information is noted in relation to the physical survey.

(i) The extent to which a family owns the house, or rents the house should be determined. The rents actually paid should be noted, for it is feasible that many could afford to amortize a low-income house or pay rent for a low-income apartment, if such were provided by the authorities.

The environmental sanitation aspects are conducted on a standardized procedure laid out by the medical profession.

Synthesizing the data

Before either the qualitative or quantitative assessment of existing conditions can be undertaken, norms or standards need to be established by the local authority for all phases of the process of recuperation or rehabilitation. Acceptability levels of the physical condition of buildings, supply of public services, utilization of human resources, levels and conditions of living, and the social cohesion of the families all need to be clearly defined. Superimposing these norms or standards (including the policy of site utilization conceived within the master-plan by the local government) over the above maps and information will reveal those physical and social institutions, buildings, or entities which are worthy of preservation, or which are available for utilization in any redevelopment scheme.

The extent of self-sufficiency of the community, both social and economic, will be revealed; and so also will be the deficiencies in the life of the families and the community as a whole.

The age-structure of the community will indicate the number of young married couples, and the likely increase of population over the coming years.

From the synthesis, and in discussions between the planners of the redevelopment project and the leaders of the squatter community, a final plan of action can then be compiled, adopted, and implemented. This plan will involve capital outlays and loans, engineering and construction works, and environmental sanitation, in which the occupants can contribute a substantial amount of the labour, the upgrading of human resources, in which the local authority can provide the skilled community leaders, and the promotion of industrial activity and employment.

BIBLIOGRAPHY

Bibliography

ABRAMS, CHARLES. *The City Is the Frontier*. New York: Harper and Row, 1967.

――――. *Squatter Settlements: The Problem and Opportunities*. (I.M.E., No. 63, Department of Housing and Urban Development.) Washington, D.C.: 1966.

CIPOLLA, C. M. *Economic History of World Population*. ("Pelican.") Harmondsworth, Middlesex: Penguin.

CLARKE, WILLIAM M. *The City in the World Economy*. ("Pelican.") Harmondsworth, Middlesex: Penguin.

CLINARD, MARSHALL B. *Slums and Community Development: Experiments in Self-Help*. New York: Free Press, 1966.

COLE, G. D. H. *The Life of Robert Owen*. London: F. Cass, 1965.

CUNHA, EUCLIDES DA. *Rebellion in the Backlands*. 1910.

DREWNOWSKI, JAN. *Social and Economic Factors in Development: Introductory Considerations on Their Meaning, Measurement and Interdependence*. (United Nations Research Institute for Social Development, Report No. 3.) Geneva: 1966.

DREWNOWSKI and SCOTT. *The Level of Living Index*. (United Nations Research Institute for Social Development, Report No. 4.) Geneva: 1966.

Ekistics: Reviews of the Problems and Science of Human Settlements. Monthly journal, published by the Athens Centre of Ekistics, P. O. Box 471, Athens, Greece.

GEDDES, SIR PATRICK. *Cities in Evolution*. London: Williams and Norgate, 1949.

GEORGE, M. DOROTHY. *London Life in the Eighteenth Century*. ("Peregrine Books.") Harmondsworth. Middlesex: Penguin.

The Complete Works of Thomas Hobbes, ed. Sir William Molesworth. 1845.

Hong Kong Annual Reports, from 1950–1960.

HONG KONG HOUSING AUTHORITY. *Annual Reports*, 1961–1965.

HOWARD, EBENEZER. *Garden Cities of Tomorrow.* London: Faber and Faber, 1946.

HOYT, HOMER. *World Urbanization.* (Urban Land Institute, Technical Bulletin, No. 43.) Washington, D.C.: Urban Land Institute.

JUPPENLATZ, M. *Housing the People in the Philippines.* (United Nations, Office of Technical Co-operation, TAO/PHIL/14, July 1968.)

————. *Urban Squatter Resettlement, Sapang Palay — A Case Study in the Philippines.* (United Nations Report — Restricted.)

KELLER, WERNER. *The Bible as History.* Translated by W. NEIL. (Illustrated.) London: Hodder and Stoughton, 1956.

KEYNES JOHN MAYNARD. *General Theory of Employment, Interest and Money.* New York: Harcourt, Brace and World, 1936.

LE PLAY, FRÉDÉRIC P. G. *La Constitution essentielle de l'humanité.*

————. *The Organization of Labour in Accordance with Custom and Law.* English translation by Herbertson.

LOCK, MAX, AND PARTNERS. *Kaduna, 1917–1967–2017: A Survey and Plan of Kaduna and Its Capital Territory, Nigeria.* London: Faber and Faber, 1966.

MALTHUS, THOMAS ROBERT. *First Essay on Population, 1798.* A reprint in facsimile of *An Essay on the Principle of Population As It Affects the Future Improvement of Society* (1798). London: Macmillan, 1966.

MANGIN, WILLIAM. "Latin American Squatter Settlements; a Problem and a Solution", *Latin American Research Review,* Vol. II, No. 3 (Summer 1967).

————. "Squatter Settlements", *Scientific American* (October 1967), pp. 21–29.

MUMFORD, LEWIS. *The City in History.* Harmondsworth, Middlesex: Penguin.

NURSKE, RAGNAR. *Problems of Capital Formation in Underdeveloped Countries.* New York: Oxford University Press, 1964.

ORAM, N. D. "Health, Housing and Urban Development", *Architecture in Australia* (November 1966). (Reprint from the *Papua and New Guinea Medical Journal* [September 1965].)

OWEN, ROBERT. *The Life of Robert Owen, Written by Himself.* London: E. Wilson, 1857.

————. *A New View of Society, or Essays on the Principle of the Formation of Human Character.* 1813.

OWEN, ROBERT DALE. *Threading My Way: Twenty-Seven Years of Autobiography.* 1874.

ROUSSEAU, JEAN JACQUES. *The Social Contract and Discourses.* Translated by G. D. H. Cole. London: Dent.

Scientific American (special edition on urbanization, September 1965).

SIMON, HERBERT A. *Models of Man.* New York: John Wiley and Sons, 1957.

TOYNBEE, ARNOLD JOSEPH. *A Study of History.* (Abridged version abridged by D. Somervell.) London: Oxford University Press, 1963.

TREVELYAN, G. M. *Illustrated English Social History.* ("Pelican.") Vol. IV. Harmondsworth, Middlesex: Penguin.

TURNER, JOHN C. *Uncontrolled Urban Settlements: Problems and Policies.* (Report for the United Nations Seminar on Urbanization.) Pittsburg: 1966.

UNITED NATIONS. *Reports of the United Nations Committee on Housing, Building and Planning,* since 1963.

———. *World Social Situation.* (Section on Latin America.) New York: 1963.

———, Department of Economic and Social Affairs. *Urbanization; Development Policies and Planning.* (International Social Development Review, No. 1.) New York: United Nations, 1968.

———. *World Population Prospects, As Assessed in 1963.* (Population Studies, No. 41.) New York: United Nations, 1966.

WARRENDER, HOWARD. *The Political Philosophy of Hobbes.* London: Oxford University Press, 1957.

WEINER, N. *Cybernetics.* Cambridge, Mass.: MIT Press, 1948.

———. *Human Use of Human Beings.* New York: Avon Books, 1950.

WOOLLEY, SIR LEONARD. *The Sumerians.* New York: Norton.

INDEX

Index